Sherlock Holmes Versus Artificial Intelligence

The Race to Solve a Murder Mystery

By

Howard J. Rankin

Cover design by Barbara Morello.

Acknowledgements

Thank you, Grant, Michael, Peter and Rich for your support and input into this project.

I also thank Karen Alley for her exceptional editing.

Thanks to my neighbors, who unknowingly offered their first names for numerous characters.

Finally, thanks and much love to my beautiful wife M.J. for her editing suggestions, patience and support.

In the early 1920s my maternal grandmother, Mary Lincoln-Wright, was the pianist for an ensemble that played at the Royal Bath Hotel in Bournemouth, an aristocratic retreat on the British south coast. While entertaining these upscale guests she met many influential people including Lawrence of Arabia and Sir Arthur Conan Doyle, the creator of Sherlock Holmes.

As a Brit and with my grandmother's indirect connection to Arthur Conan Doyle, I have always been fascinated by the Holmes character, and even more so as I ventured into the science of how we do, or don't think and the mysterious complexity of consciousness.

This is a novel, a fictional mystery. However, some things within this book are true to life. Some of the information is indeed an accurate accounting of different research on criminal behavior and violent crime. These sources have been included in the appendix. Also, references to myself, Grant Renier, and IntualityAI reflect reality. IntualityAI is a predictive analytics company based in North Carolina, and I work there as the Science Director, while Grant Renier is the founder.

All other persons and events are fictional and any resemblance or similarity to persons living, or dead is purely coincidental.

***

Sherlock Holmes was born in August 1854 and had a very intelligent brother called Mycroft, who worked in government intelligence. Sherlock was rarely interested in women except one called Irene Adler but there's no record of him ever marrying. The Holmes family tradition thus lay upon the shoulders, and other anatomical parts, of Mycroft.

Mycroft had a son in 1879 called George, and George had son of his own, Edward in 1920. Edward was fascinated, even obsessed, by his great uncle's fame and abilities and studied Sherlock's talents and achievements with immense passion. Thus, it was no surprise that when Edward and his wife Julia were expecting their first child after several miscarriages and were sure the baby would be a girl, they decided to name it Shirley. However, they were wrong and the baby turned out to be a boy and, of course, there was no other choice but to name him Sherlock.

The young Sherlock, genetically and psychologically connected to his great grandfather's brother, and inspired by his father's obsession with the famed detective, was determined from an early age to enter the world of detection. He followed in his great grandfather's brother's footsteps emulating his career and special skills.

When he started up his detective business in London in the 1980s, Sherlock knew he needed the help of a medical doctor and as luck would have it, a good friend of his was indeed medically qualified. His friend's name was Watt Johnson but during an apparent episode of dyslexia, he changed it to Dr. John Watson when he joined his friend Sherlock's detective business.

Many people believed that Sherlock was indeed an exact replica of the original detective, but was that just wishful thinking or some combination of genetic and experiential mysticism? There was no question that this Sherlock physically resembled his older relative, and was not shy about wearing similar clothes, especially a deerstalker hat, a hundred years after the peak of their popularity. And he also took a flat in Baker Street from where he ran his private investigator business.

For those who knew the family history, Sherlock had been
resurrected.

■■■

Artificial Intelligence

Artificial Intelligence (AI) has rapidly evolved in recent years, transforming numerous aspects of our lives. This revolutionary field encompasses a wide range of technologies and applications that simulate human intelligence in machines. The application spans the use of AI in answering customer service calls (yes, your call is very important to us, please wait for the next available representative) to sophisticated hacking of sensitive governmental and military information.

AI has demonstrated immense potential across various domains, including health care, finance, transportation, entertainment, and spying. In health care, AI algorithms can analyze vast amounts of medical data to assist in diagnosing diseases, identifying treatment options, and predicting patient outcomes. This has the potential to revolutionize medical care and improve patient outcomes.

However, the rapid advancement of AI also brings challenges and concerns. Ethical considerations such as data privacy, algorithmic biases, and job displacement require careful attention. It is crucial to develop and implement ethical frameworks to ensure AI technologies are used responsibly and equitably.

Additionally, the potential risks associated with AI, such as unintended consequences and the lack of transparency in complex algorithms, raise concerns about accountability and decision making. Striking the right balance between technological advancement and ethical considerations is essential for the responsible development and deployment of AI.

Main characters:

Shane Kenwight: Chief

Earl Bestinnie: Science Director

Nat Gurnal: Artificial Intelligence Specialist

Rob Shine: Robotics Expert

Ron McFerie: Govt Liaison

Rue Carime: Chief Adminstrator

Mary Heald: Bioengineering:

Sandra: Night Receptionist

Allison: Day Receptionist

Dave and Khang: Night Security Guards

Sherlock Holmes, Dr. John Watson: Investigators

Jim Faulkner and Colleen Williams: MI6 investigators

Jay Pugastan: Medical expert

Introduction

It's a time of uncertainty. China has just invaded Taiwan and there is an international crisis of immense proportions.

At Bletchley in England, a secret team of AI and robotics experts run major operations, specifically decoding messages, and using AI for constant analysis, one of several teams around the world which drive the international response to the crisis. The team was assembled eighteen months ago when tensions started to run very high in the Pacific and almost a year before China invaded Taiwan. Then the Pacific was pacific no more.

There's a team of seven experts coordinating this immensely important operation but just as the conflict intensifies, something dramatic happens. One of the team is found dead.

The investigation begins, and Sherlock Holmes is called in to solve the mystery. Questions abound:

Was the AI system hacked and programmed to kill?

Was it one of his associates on the Bletchley team?

Was it a robot acting on its own?

Did the person commit suicide and if so, why?

The team creates its own AI system – Noel – and expects it to solve the problem without any outside help.

Holmes and the other investigators have to dig deep into the problem of consciousness to solve the matter.

As Holmes and the Noel engineers try to piece together a logical train of events that will solve the problem and identify the murderer, if there is one, they encounter a challenge that seems to defy logic and needs a deeper insight into how the minds of robots -- and humans -- work.

About fifty miles north of London, in a village called Bletchley, you'll find the Range, a spectacular British mansion The property boasts an isolated splendor of more than 10,000 square feet, just a few kilometers from the famous Bletchley Park. That is where Alan Turing and his colleagues decisively cracked Nazi codes and by some estimates reduced World War II by two years and turned the war in the Allies' favor.

The Range still retains its splendor and boasts of eleven bedrooms, several great workspaces, community dining and meeting rooms and a basement, recently enlarged to house the main computer technology, as well as a safety bunker. The property is adjacent to a delightful lake and gardens. It is well protected by many trees and a weaponized fence largely hidden by the dazzling flora and fauna. It is perhaps a little ironic that this symbol of 19th-century British imperialism is the working place of people trying to prevent 21st century imperialism, as the Chinese aggression in the Pacific continues to send the planet into chaos. Every nation on earth is feeling the fall-out from the multiple conflicts erupting in the wake of the threat of nuclear conflict.

Here in Bletchley, a team of experts has been assembled to use their technical and scientific excellence to maximize the use of AI engineering and robots. Their mission is to use such technology for influencing and guiding political and military strategy and deciphering codes used by the Chinese and their allies. Just as Bletchley Park was the home of experts who deciphered German code in the Second World War, it was now hoped that this Bletchley-based team could turn the tide of war once again.

Chapter One

Monday: 6 p.m.

***"Sometimes emotions are more important than
rationality."***
Marco Bizzarri

"I'm delighted to tell you we made a significant difference today," said Dr. Shane Kenwight, addressing his six other colleagues. Together, they made up a team of seven experts in their field, leading hundreds of scientists around the world in an effort to defend against the Chinese.

"As you know, over the last few days Nat and his team anticipated specific Chinese moves in the South Pacific thanks to their use of AI. As a result, that information was used for strategic planning. Late this morning, the Chinese were lured into the trap and suffered many casualties and losses."

Rugged applause broke out amongst the assembled team, with Nat Gurnal receiving numerous pats on the back and hugs.

"Outstanding work, Nat!" Shane yelled over the applause. "That's why we are here!"

Nat shyly accepted the praise.

"The current estimate is that the Chinese lost more than 3,000 men," added Shane.

A buzz of surprised gratification filled the room.

The group of seven were very close. They were not just drawn together by their love and expertise in science, but for an understanding of how much Artificial Intelligence had to offer in any setting, especially in one as significant as war. And living and working together at the Range for most of the time also gave the group a social as well as an official identity.

"Can you predict when this crazy conflict will be over, Nat?" asked Mary, the bioengineering expert.

"I wish I could," replied Nat with an earnest smile directed at Mary.

"Don't we all," said Rue. She and Nat also shared a warm relationship, and he returned an awkward smile.

"Today's events will certainly hit the headlines and prompt the Chinese to investigate further so they can find out who keeps luring them into danger," Shane said. "We need to keep security watertight And let's be on our guard more than ever. We simply can't afford any leaks. Not a word to anyone."

"That is, of course, easier said than done," said Ron, the government liaison officer. "The Chinese will be trying to figure out which of the AI centers is responsible and probably target them, if not all of us. We are dependent on our colleagues outside of here to keep their damn mouths shut, and we have very little control over them."

"We can only do our best," said Mary. "We must ensure our crypto security is unbreakable. They'll continually be trying to hack us."

"So far so good," said Earl, the chief scientific advisor. "We were lucky that one time when we caught it with seconds to spare. We just have to keep the utmost vigilance."

Earl was referring to an attempted hack of the Bletchley team's software several months before. They caught it just in time, preserving their privacy as well as specific details on their modes of operation.

"Let's not forget what happened at the CIA three weeks ago," said Mary, referring to an event in which Chinese hackers had managed to access the infrastructure of the headquarters in Washington and started sending toxic fumes throughout the building.

The team nodded grimly in recognition of the important reminder.

"While we are talking about our best practices, does anyone have ideas for upgrades to any systems or operations?" asked Shane.

"Since we were just talking about keeping quiet and avoiding leaks at all costs, I have a concern," said Mary. "I know we feel we are close to our teams and know them well, but I am concerned about the odds. We have about 300 people working under us. How can we be sure that no-one is talking loosely? How can we be sure there isn't a traitor in our midst? It bothers me a lot."

The people Mary referred to were spread throughout the town of Bletchley and only rarely would they venture into the grand estate itself. Instead, they used their own offices and accommodations in different parts of the Milton Keynes area.

"These people have been vetted multiple times and they are largely kept away from us. I'm not sure there is anything more that we can do," said Shane.

"Unfortunately, there's no such thing as perfection," said Nat. "I'm not sure there's anything more that we can do either."

The team nodded their heads in collective agreement.

"Okay, well, senior security has been given the heads-up and they are increasing their vigilance both on the ground and in the air. Let's bear in mind our own measures in the event of a physical attack," said Shane. "Do we need to practice that again to be sure?"

The assembled team agreed that there was no need to physically practice their escape routine. They all knew how to access the underground bunker if necessary. Shane reminded them that security will likely sound occasional alarms as a test to ensure that they were all staying vigilant.

"Okay, then. See you all bright and early tomorrow morning when we'll evaluate any updates and news. Sleep well, people," said Shane.

The team left the room and headed off to their respective rooms hoping for a welcome night's sleep.

A good night's sleep, however, is not always an easy mission when your life is engulfed in complex science and the mission is to end a war and even save the planet. Each of the team leaders had their own way of dealing with the stress and trying to relax.

When Shane reached his bedroom on the ground floor, he looked out of his window at the beautiful lake reflecting the late sunlight and contemplated the tragedy that was this humanitarian disaster. Then, he immediately headed for the remote control and turned on the TV news.

The setback suffered by the Chinese as the result of Nat's technology was on every channel. They had lost several ships and aircraft, as well as many soldiers and sailors. There was some speculation by experts as to how the engagement had occurred, but Shane heard nothing that was anywhere close to the truth: that a sophisticated AI system based in the U.K. was the basis of the strategic success.

As he let out a sigh of relief, his mind turned to the recent discussion in the team meeting.

Vulnerability. Without any premeditation he was aware of a thought: If he were indeed to lose one member of his team, who would it be? Without exploring it further, he refocused his attention on the TV screen and tried to forget the ghostly question.

Two rooms away on the ground floor, Ron was also considering the meeting while having a quick snack. He mused over the brief celebration of Nat, following the revelation of the AI prediction that deceived the Chinese. He felt a little irritated that Nat was getting all the plaudits when he himself, had played a major role in convincing his military supervisors that the AI output needed to be acted on. Still, he appreciated Nat and scoffed at his own pettiness, and settled down to distract himself by watching some soccer.

In one of the luxurious bedrooms upstairs, Rue, watched a romantic movie. As two characters signaled their attraction to each other, she immediately remembered the rare smile that Nat had given her after she had praised his effort. She drifted off to sleep, the stress of the day replaced with pleasant thoughts. But a nightmare woke her up suddenly. She could only remember the feelings of the nightmare not the details. But she was in some unknown rural area and felt terrified. It confused her but she eventually was able to get back to sleep before daylight dawned.

Nat also reviewed the day's events in his room. But rather than feeling pleased at his ability to use his analytic skills to program AI predictions, he was questioning his abilities. His characteristically harsh self-examination had often led to new creative ideas, but on this occasion, it left him feeling more than a little depressed. Anyone who knew him would not be able to understand this genius's self-deprecation. He tried to distract himself by scanning social media platforms, which were full of comments and opinions about the war.

Rob spent some of the evening musing about the incredible technology that he had helped build. He often wondered what the robots and the software were doing when the limited night staff were on duty. On this evening he wondered whether the AI system would be secretly upset that Nat got all the credit for the recent victory over the Chinese. There was part of Rob who seriously entertained the notion that the robots were sentient. He amused himself thinking about what they would indeed do if they were angry. Would they simply sulk and stop cooperating, or would they be more aggressive? Would they, for example, interfere with the environment in some way, like what happened at the CIA headquarters?

Rob smiled to himself at the thoughts of such events and the implications. If robots were sentient, they would ultimately need some sort of psychotherapy. Feelings could easily confuse even artificial intelligence, in the way that they interfere with human logic. If that were the case Rob wondered whether artificial intelligence machines were in love with their opposite gender "parent" as Freud suggested. Or did these machines worship their makers, as humans did gods? Eventually, Rob dismissed this train of thought and distracted himself with some crossword puzzles.

Mary often had similar thoughts about artificial intelligence. Could these systems operate on their own and even defy their programming? Could they create havoc inadvertently? Or intentionally? Mary understood that some of the AI processes were very similar to animal biology and had even presented a keynote address at a major bioengineering conference on how such processes imply the development of sentience.

Mary was also impressed by the work of Hubert Dreyfus, a Massachusetts Institute of Technology and University of California professor of philosophy who back in the 1960s wrote a paper titled "Why robots must have bodies in order to be intelligent." Dreyfus's view was that skills and action preceded knowledge, not the other way round. Mary often struggled to accommodate modern robotics with Dreyfus's notion. She reflected on what the concept of intelligence actually meant. She also liked to repeat the quote of Alan Turing who had helped crack the Nazi Enigma Code in World War II at Bletchley Park, just down the road.

"If a machine is expected to be infallible, it can't also be intelligent."

The scientific advisor, Earl Bestinnie, was appreciated for his outstanding intelligence. In fact, in an unusually sexist remark, Earl once whispered to Nat that he was twice as smart as Mary Hedlar and Rue Carime combined. "The equation is $E(Earl) = M(Mary) \times C(Carime)^2$," joked Earl. Nat wasn't impressed, which made Earl reflect on Nat's relationship, if any, with these two smart, attractive women and with the opposite sex generally.

Earl was an enigmatic genius who believed that imagination was far more important than knowledge. His creativity was astounding and often led to enthusiastic debates amongst the team members who completely valued Earl's imagination.

As the sunset on the Range, each person was lost in their own thoughts. Little did they know that when daylight emerged again, their lives would be forever changed.

Chapter Two

Tuesday: 7:30 a.m.

"We're blind to our blindness. We have very little idea of how little we know. We're not designed to know how little we know."
Daniel Kahneman

As usual, the team gathered in the conference room with tea and coffee to get the latest updates on the war. Most of the news was about the damage inflicted on the Chinese in the AI inspired maneuver.

Shane, the first to arrive, was relieved to find out that there was no hint of the Bletchley involvement in the news or outside of it. Ron arrived shortly afterwards and reinforced the reassuring updated bulletins.

"I've spoken with headquarters, and they have picked up nothing about our involvement," Ron said defiantly. "Let's see what Nat comes up with next. This could be pivotal."

Shane nodded and looked up to see Rue step through the door.

"Good morning, Boss," Rue said with her usual determined smile. "Everything good?"

"So far," replied Shane.

Earl arrived shortly after Rue.

"Did you sleep well?" Ron asked somewhat cynically.

Earl rolled his eyes, which he could do better than closing them for sleep. The team all knew of Earl's insomnia, which often was the setting for some very creative ideas.

"Actually," Earl started, "While I was awake, I did have an idea. I need to talk to Nat about it."

"Fancy that, Earl, you having an idea," joked Shane.

Before long Mary and Rob arrived and shared the usual morning pleasantries with the other team members.

"Okay gang, get your breakfast, it's time to start," Shane said.

"Nat's not here yet," Rue pointed out.

"Let's give it five more minutes then," Shane said.

The time passed and Nat had still not appeared.

"He's probably having breakfast with that robot of his," said Mary, half seriously. "Or scrolling through social media."

"Let's get started. We know that Nat isn't always the greatest timekeeper," said Shane.

The experts were still weighing the impact of the Chinese defeat, Shane reported, and the Chief of Staff were asking for more predictions to consolidate the gains.

Ron's phone vibrated on the table. He moved to the back of the room to answer it. The group used this time to break and refill their teacups.

"I wonder where Nat is," Mary said. "I know he gets distracted and forgets what time it is, but it's not like him to be this late."

"I know, I'm started to get a little worried," Rue said.

Ron called for their attention. He looked serious.

"That was HQ. They have just intercepted a message which suggests that the Chinese are starting to work out that we were the ones who inspired the attack. They are gaining more info on exactly who we are," Ron said.

A collective murmur of frustration and distress ricocheted around the room.

"Come on, people," said Shane. "We all knew that this was a possibility if not likely at some point or another. This will not stop us. In fact, let's use it to push as faster."

"The one guy who needs to know this the most isn't even here," Rob said.

"Yes, where the hell is he? He's never been this late before," said Earl.

"I'll call him," said Shane, picking up his phone. "No reply."

"Someone needs to wake him up," said Earl.

"I'll go," volunteered Ron.

"Wait, I'll come with you," said Rue as she followed Ron out of the door to the grand staircase that led up to Nat's bedroom.

The others returned to the serious matter of their exposure.

"We anticipated the Chinese would start to figure out what happened," said Shane trying to reassure his colleagues. "Everything is in place to keep us safe. We just need to stay vigilant and ensure we enforce the protocols to the letter."

Up the grand staircase and a few yards to the right, Ron and Rue had reached Nat's room.

"Nat, it's time to wake up!" shouted Ron as he banged heavily on the door.

He repeated the action more loudly when there was no reply.

"Nat are you okay?" asked Rue through the door.

Still no reply.

"I have the master key," said Ron, pulling a key ring from his jacket pocket.

Down in the conference room, the rest of the team was trying to adjust to the news about their exposure.

"I've always assumed this would happen," said Shane. "It shouldn't make a difference to us. It doesn't to me."

Shane was interrupted by his phone's ringtone.

"It's Ron," he said to the others as he answered it.

"How's Nat? Is he up yet?" Shane half-joked.

Within a second Shane's expression had changed into one of disbelief.

"What?!" he yelled into the phone.

Shane put down the phone on the table in a solemn movement.

"What is it?" said Mary.
Shane spoke.

"It's Nat. He's dead."

Chapter Three

Tuesday 8:00 a.m.

"Intuition will tell the thinking mind where to look next."
Jonas Salk

The solemn news of Nat's death overwhelmed the room like nuclear fallout.

After a moment to process the news, the questions started to erupt.

"Has this got anything to do with the recent events in the war?" wondered Rue aloud.

"Could it have been an accident?" asked Mary.

"I hate to say this but isn't suicide a possibility?" said Rob.

"We don't know. That's why we have to get on this immediately! We must get to the bottom of it!" yelled Shane stressfully.

"First, let's get the medical team on it right away," said Earl, who like his colleagues was shaken by the traumatic event.

"Ron are you still there?" Shane asked into his phone.

"Yes, I'm here."

"We need to get the medical team there right now!"

"They have just arrived," said Ron. "They're examining him right now."

Jay Pugastan performed an examination of Nat's body. Ron felt confident in Jay's ability, as he was a brilliant emergency physician who had worked with Indian security teams for many years and had even been featured on television shows about medicine, health and wellness. He was excellent at reaching quick and accurate evaluations about the cause of death. Speed is often of the essence in such cases. Dr. Jay had also taught his team the nuances of situational diagnoses, which involved not only examining the body but also the environment in which it was found.

"Doctor, can you head down to the conference room and tell them of your initial findings?" asked Ron. No sooner had he finished the question, the good doctor was on his way.

When Dr Jay entered the conference room, he felt the collective shock and anxiety of the leadership team. They immediately asked him how Nat had died.

Dr. Pugastan didn't hold back.

"Our good friend and servant, Nat," he hesitated for a dramatic moment, then continued, "was poisoned."

Gasps of surprise and shock ricocheted around the room.

"How?" asked Shane.

"Well, that's the key question," said the doctor. "It may have been administered to him directly, or he took it, either inadvertently or deliberately. Our estimate is that the time of death was around midnight to one in the morning."

"Who could have done that to him?" asked Earl.

"It could have been any of you, anyone else who works here, an outside agency…anyone, including Nat himself," said Dr. Pugastan.

"You're not suggesting one of us killed Nat?" asked Rue in disbelief.

"I have learned that in any investigation, no-one can be ruled out until they have been ruled out," said Dr. Jay.

The room went stressfully quiet. As if the previous day's events hadn't been dramatic enough, these leaders were all now persons of interest in Nat's death.

"That's ridiculous," said Earl. "Why on earth would any of us want to kill Nat!?"

"Of course, Earl. I know it seems ridiculous," said Shane. "But it does mean that we need our ultimate bosses, MI6, to investigate Nat's death. We can't be the ones to do it."

"Well, as you're already under the aegis of MI6, they will get involved right away," said Dr. Jay. "May I make a suggestion. You might consider starting with an expert rather than the agency."

"Do you have any suggestions or recommendations, doctor?" asked Ron who had arrived back on the scene to be part of the deliberations.

"Actually, I do," the medic said.

"Who is it?" Shane asked.

There was a brief pause as Dr. Jay pondered how to proceed.

"Do you remember the Heathrow heist, the Piccadilly bombing, and the Manchester mass shooting?"

The group nodded their heads.

"Well, this guy solved all of those crimes. And may I say so, he did it brilliantly," said the doctor.

"That's Shylock somebody or another, isn't it?" opined Mary.

"Almost," said the doctor. "It's Holmes, Sherlock Holmes," he corrected Mary.

"Isn't he a bit long in the tooth now?" Shane asked.

"Maybe, but he is still brilliant," said Dr. Jay.

"Does this Holmes guy know anything about technology?" asked Earl.

"No, I don't think he uses it much, if at all," said the doctor.

"Well, that's absurd," Earl shouted. "Here we are at the forefront of technology, facing a major problem, and we won't be using any technology to solve it!" proclaimed Earl indignantly.

The others echoed their agreement with Earl. Surely their advanced computing and analytical skills should have a part to play in the solution of the problem of who killed Nat.

"If we're going to have to choose between an old investigator and current technology, give me the latter any time," said Mary to murmurs of support from her colleagues.

"Soon enough MI6 are going to be involved. Perhaps we should just hand it over to them and let them decide how to proceed?" said Shane.

"MI6 know about our technology and what we are able to do with it but how good are they at solving specific situations like this one," said Earl. "And as doc says, their involvement will slow the whole process down."

"What a freaking dilemma," Rue said.

There was a pause. Each of the group was deep in thought as they sought the right way forward.

Eventually, Shane spoke.

"Well, we need to avoid binary thinking," said Shane enacting his role as the leader.

"How about this?"

The group waited for the leader's words of wisdom.

"Let's alert MI6 now, if they haven't been told already, and ask for permission to get this Holmes guy started on the case. This will be our official plan and policy. Then separately and informally, we can set up our own robotics and AI programming to solve the problem using whatever data is available to us, including Mr. Holmes, if he is willing to cooperate with us."

"Good idea, Shane," said Rob. "I can get us started right away. Of course, Nat's expertise will be sadly missed. However, if a version of his advanced AI can solve his murder, that will be sweet revenge indeed and a great irony."

The others agreed, even Dr. Pugastan.

"Don't forget you can always engage some other AI experts to help," said Dr. Jay.

"Yes, of course, We have several of those here who worked under Nat. We will definitely involve them," said Earl.

"Doctor, do you have anyone in mind? You seem to know many experts in these relevant fields," asked Ron.

"Actually, I do. I was thinking of one person in particular, so if you need me to make the connection, just let me know," said Dr. Jay. "In the meantime, I will introduce you, Shane, to this Holmes fellow and you can get started."

"I'll get in touch with M16 to get their permission to get Holmes involved immediately," Ron said.

The room fell silent again. It seemed unreal and inconceivable that Nat was gone, a horrible nightmare that, they hoped, would suddenly vanish and restore the vastly better and comfortable reality that had existed just a few minutes earlier. If only life were that easy and convenient.

Chapter Four

Tuesday: 1pm

"It is through science that we prove, but through intuition that we discover."
Henri Poincare

Dr. Watson arrived home from a long morning at King's College Hospital in south London where he had been giving a seminar on alimentary diseases. He was not surprised to see Sherlock sitting in the living room, staring into the fireplace, and smoking his pipe.

"What's happening my friend?" said Watson cheerfully.

There was a short silence before Sherlock looked up and responded.

"I have just been offered an interesting assignment, Watson."

His friend looked at him with inquisitive grin.

"There's been a possible murder at that Bletchley place, and they want me there immediately to investigate."

"Bletchley, where they have all those robots and artificial intelligence systems?" asked Watson.

"Yes, I believe it is an annex to the Bletchley you are talking about. But in any case, why can't they have their damn robots figure out who committed the murder, if that's what it is? After all, everyone knows that AI is vastly superior to any human," he said.

Watson didn't catch the sarcasm in Holmes' voice.

"Come on, Holmes, they simply don't have the expansive consciousness to work out the complex details of any crime. Don't be discouraged by the prospect of having to take on technology. You can beat any robot."

"I know you're right, Watson. But suppose artificial intelligence solves the crime before I do? What then? My reputation will be ruined. Beaten by a darned computer!"

"You're being too hard on yourself," said Watson, and he meant it. Watson was impressed with the advance of technology, but he was still convinced that it could not compete with human intelligence, especially in solving complex problems, like crimes.

Holmes responded. "You know how much I dislike all this tech hype. Even after IBM named their computer after you, Watson, I didn't think they could compete with real human intelligence."

"Well, Holmes, here's your chance to prove your point. If you beat the computer, surely that will enhance your reputation even more?"

"You have a point there, Watson," said Holmes pensively. "Perhaps IBM or some other tech outfit will name their next computer after me," Holmes said with a contemplative expression and the emphasis on the "me."

"And the income is sure to be good and will probably pay for that ritzy cruise you've been talking about," said Watson.

Sherlock welcomed that idea with wide smile, which prompted his colleague to respond.

"Does that mean we're off to Bletchley?" asked Watson.

"I'm never one to refuse a challenge. And this will help me get a better understanding of how people expect to use AI to disrupt our business, the business of solving a crime. Okay. Yes, let me call them back and tell them we'll be there in a couple of hours. Do you have the time to accompany me there or do you have lectures or seminars to give over the next few days?"

"I'm clear for the rest of the week! It will be a good change of pace to get out of the city," said Watson.

Within a few minutes Holmes was on a call with the Bletchley hierarchy.

"Dr. Kenwight, it would be an honor and a privilege to help you solve this dastardly mystery."

Shane was excited to hear the news.

"That's great! When will you be here?"

"My assistant, Dr. Watson, and I will be there in about a couple of hours. Please ensure that nothing, and I mean nothing, is removed from the crime scene."

"Fantastic Mr. Holmes. Nat's body is currently in one of our special labs and I'm sure that nothing else has been removed from his room. You come with the highest of recommendations and I'm thrilled you have accepted the offer. You will need to sign some papers. As you know, this is a delicate matter of great international significance. Can I send over papers you need to sign before we get started? I can fax them to you, right now."

"I don't have a fax," said Holmes.

"Can I email them to you?"

"No. I don't use email very much. I can sign them when I get there. Will that be okay?"

"Yes, of course," said Shane. Fortunately, as this was not a virtual interaction, Sherlock couldn't see the concerned frown on Shane's face.

"Okay, then. We will see you in a couple of hours. Should I call this number if I need to reach you?" asked Holmes.

"Yes, that would be fine. See you in a couple of hours," replied Shane.

Shane put the phone down pensively. He turned to Ron who was in the office.

"I hope we haven't made a mistake with this Holmes guy. He doesn't have a fax, hardly uses email -- how the hell will he solve a mystery that might involve AI?"

"I guess he will use SHI instead," said Ron.

There was a pause while Shane deciphered Ron's proffered initials. "SHI? Oh, I get it," said Shane with a triumphant grin. "SHI equals Sherlock Holmes Investigations!"

"No," said Ron.

He then quickly corrected Shane.

"SHI means sensory human intelligence."

Chapter Five

Tuesday: 4:15pm

"If everyone is thinking alike, then somebody isn't thinking."
George S. Patton

The investigators arrived at The Range in the small town of Bletchley a little after four in the afternoon. The town was in the Milton Keynes area of Buckinghamshire, with a population of just more than a quarter of a million people.

The security guard on the gate at the edge of the property had been prepared for their arrival and after checking the investigators credentials let them into the grand estate. Watson drove slowly down a scenic driveway that led to the mansion. Watson and Holmes were both impressed by the majesty of the property, especially the shimmering lake surrounded by magnificent trees and beautifully manicured gardens.

As they drove up to the mansion, they were immediately received by Shane Kenwight and Ron, who quickly guided them into the main office to go through the formalities of signing the necessary papers.

The group headed through the main door and entered a sparkling large foyer that had spectacular winding staircase to the right. After depositing their coats with the valet, Shane led them into a large office and invited the investigators.

"Have a seat," Shane said as he pulled out the document for the two to sign.

Watson was reading the documents, but Holmes barely glanced at them, only checking the compensation details, and signing where necessary. Sherlock was very eager to get to the crime scene, knowing every second could make a difference to the investigation. When all the signatures were registered, Shane stood up.

"I know you are in a hurry to get to the crime scene, but first, let me show you to your rooms," Shane said. "We assumed you might want to stay the night, or even longer, and have prepared a couple of rooms here in this delightful building," said Shane.

"Well, thank you. That is most helpful. We'll drop off our bags and get started," said Sherlock.

Holmes and Watson were led to their assigned rooms which were adjacent to each other. They were both impressed by the majesty of the bedrooms; the satin curtains, bronzed chandeliers, and inviting leather sofas. The view from the windows was spectacular, transcending the delightful tree branches and extending to the glistening lake beyond. However, this wasn't the time to admire the view. Sherlock dropped his luggage and perused the room carefully once more before leaving to meet Watson, Dr. Shane, and Ron.

Once the four met up, Shane could see Holmes was still very edgy and wanted access to the crime scene.

"Let's go, then," Shane said. "Once there we'll leave you alone, I promise."

"Well, we might check in with you and ask to connect with Noel once he's up and running," said Shane, qualifying his statement.

"Noel?" Holmes asked.

"Our AI system that we hope can help with the investigation," said Ron.

Holmes flashed a sardonic look at Watson. Then turned to Ron.

"We'll be delighted to meet …him," said Holmes unconvincingly.

Once Shane guided them to the crime scene, Holmes and Watson quickly set about their investigation of Nat's room.

They studied the doorway and couldn't detect any sign of forced entry. They checked the windows and saw that they were all locked, with no sign of anything out of place. They investigated the environment carefully and found no obvious clues. They discovered what they assumed was Nat's phone and checked it for any fingerprints. Watson volunteered to unlock the phone and check any recent activity once he got back to his room and could access the relevant technology.

They had explored the crime scene for about fifteen minutes when Dr. Rob knocked on the door.

"I just wanted to introduce myself. I'm the robotics expert of this team, and the programmer of Noel," Rob said.

"Nice to meet you," Watson said, as Holmes looked on warily.

"Noel is up and running. I hate to interrupt but I think this would be a good time for you to meet him," said Rob.

Before Holmes had time to vent his cynicism, Watson chimed in.

"We'd be honored. Come on, Holmes, let's go and meet Noel."

Rob led the two investigators down to the basement where Noel was waiting for them.

"Dr. Rob, who else has access to Noel? You understand that everyone here, including yourself, is potentially a suspect and certainly a person of interest," asked Sherlock.

"Dr. Shane, our MI6 bosses, and I have discussed this in detail. Only I will have access to Noel until this matter is settled. I will be the only one to monitor the programming so that the fundamental workings of Noel will remain the same. I will be the only one to devise programs that will allow Noel to do whatever research is necessary. And I will be the only one to provide more information as it becomes available."

"Are you sure of that?" asked Watson.

"As sure as I can be," said Dr. Rob.

Holmes looked cynically at Rob as he finished speaking.

"We have some very clever people here, Mr. Holmes, so I can't say with certainty that no-one will have access. But I'm 99% sure that is the case."

"I guess we'll have to make do with that," said Holmes.

And with that Rob introduced the investigators to Noel.

"It's a pleasure to meet you both, Dr. Watson and Mr. Holmes," Noel stated in a slightly slow and unexpressive voice.

"Ah, I see you speak perfect robot English," said Holmes sarcastically.

Noel had the perfect answer to Holmes's cynicism. He ignored it completely and continued.

"Have you any information for me that could be useful?" Noel continued.

Dr. Rob noted Sherlock's rather bored expression at this announcement and quickly intervened.

"Mr. Holmes, we are hoping that our technology could assist in your investigation. It can access and process millions of bits of information far quicker than any human can. It can also correlate important variables and provide insights that might remain invisible to the human mind. I do believe that Noel can be very helpful in your investigation. So, I invite you to please share with us any information that Noel can process to help you," said Rob.

"Actually, we have found a few items of interest."

"Will you be so kind as to share them with me?" Noel replied.

Watson shot Holmes a quizzical glance and immediately wondered what Holmes was up to. He didn't have to wait long to find out.

Holmes faced the robot and began.

"Well, Dr. Nat was poisoned. We're not sure exactly what the poison is at the moment, but we will find that out shortly."

"I also found a mouse, with large black ears, who seemed to be carrying some sort of poison, that likely killed him, too," Holmes continued.

Watson shot Holmes an even more quizzical glance, but that didn't deter him from continuing.

"We also found some sort of ticket that appears emanated from Orlando, Florida, in the United States. And near the dead rodent the initials W.D. were drawn. What do you make of it, Noel?"

There was a pause.

"*I think I have identified the perpetrator*," said Noel in an unassuming manner.

"Please tell me who it is?" pleaded Sherlock, as Rob and Watson looked on in surprise.

There was a pause, then Noel spoke.

"*W.D, is Walt Disney and his arena, Disneyworld is in Orlando in the U.S. state of Florida. The rodent had large black ears. Therefore, based on this information, there's only one conclusion*," asserted Noel.

The three humans waited with bated breath for the AI robot's pronouncement.

"*The killer is Mickey Mouse.*"

"Ah, you see Watson," said Sherlock triumphantly, "These machines are only as good as the information humans give them. They're not even intelligent!"

"What motive would someone have for killing Mickey Mouse and Dr. Nat?" asked Holmes turning his focus back to the machine. "*I'm not sure of that*," replied Noel, "*But I would definitely interview Minnie Mouse if I were you.*"

Watson shrugged. Rob looked flustered. Before Holmes could continue, Noel spoke again.

"However," said Noel, *"Mickey Mouse is merely a fictional character and therefore can't be the perpetrator. Rather, you are playing tricks on me and giving me useless information, Mr.
Holmes."*

"Maybe I am," replied Holmes, "But some human gave you that information, too, so I'm not that impressed."

Noel continued.

"Did you know Mr. Holmes, that the Pest Control Service was here just a few hours before Nat's death? Perhaps you should research what pesticides they use and whether that poor rodent, if there really was one, was poisoned by some chemical used by the pest control service?"

Watson saw Rob stifling a wry smile as Holmes thought about his reply.

"What's the name of the Pest Control company?" Sherlock asked Noel.

"Natural Exterminators," replied Noel, quickly adding, *"An interesting name don't you think under the circumstances?"*

"Ah, if solving a crime were that simple," said Holmes.

"Don't underestimate these AI robots, Mr. Holmes. They have access to millions of bits of information," said Rob.

"Don't underestimate humans Dr. Rob. As Dr. Watson here will no doubt confirm, we humans have billions of cells sharing information with each other all the time. And it allows us to do things that Noel cannot do – like taste and smell and even have gut feelings."

"I would appreciate that you treat Noel and the concept of Artificial Intelligence with respect, otherwise…" said Rob before being abruptly cut off.

"Otherwise, what?" said Holmes aggressively.

"I will give you a piece of my mind!" said Rob loudly, staring directly onto Holmes' eyes.

"Well, if I have a choice of which piece of your mind I get, can I request the pre-frontal cortex. It seems to be the most optimal of your brain structures as I'm currently questioning the functionality of your limbic system," said Holmes.

"I said a piece of my mind, not brain!!" shouted Rob.

"What's the difference?" asked Holmes rather dismissively.

Rob stopped and took a deep breath.

"All I ask Sherlock is that you respect artificial intelligence," said Rob with a softening tone.

"Is it artificial or superficial intelligence?" asked Holmes, whereupon Watson grabbed him by the waist and directed him out the door.

"Thank you, Noel and Dr. Rob. We will get back to the scene and tell you what we find," said Watson forcefully guiding Holmes out of the room.

Chapter Six

Tuesday 5:30pm

"It is not rational to assume, without evidence, that rationality can disclose everything about the world, just because it can disclose some things. Our intuition in favor of rationality, where we are inclined to use it, is just that - an intuition. Reason is founded in intuition and ends in intuition, like a pair of massive bookends."
Iain McGilchrist

Watson and Holmes were silent as they went back up the grand staircase to the murder scene. Watson only released his grip on Holmes once they had entered Nat's bedroom and closed the door.

"Holmes don't be so openly dismissive of these robots and the concept of AI. I have to admit, Noel might be helpful."

"I accept that, but I don't accept that Noel can therefore connect all the dots in a meaningful way. I think humans are better at that. Well, at least some of us," said Holmes defiantly.

"Well, I thought the information about the pest control service that Noel gave us was potentially very useful," said Watson.

"Maybe, but we easily could have got that information ourselves. Let's check on that and find out the precise details of their visit."

"Yes, of course," said Watson.

"But first I want you to examine Nat's body more thoroughly. I'm not yet certain that poison was the instrument of his death." "Well, didn't you tell Noel and Dr. Rob that Nat was poisoned?" questioned Watson.

"I also told them that Micky Mouse was the murderer," said Sherlock with a serious scowl.

"Let's not forget that Dr. Rob himself is a person of interest. I'm certainly not going to reveal all my thoughts on the matter to him or Noel," added Sherlock.

"So, you're not sure whether poison was the instrument of murder or even a possible suicide?" asked Watson.

"No, not yet."

"Do you have any basis for your doubts, other than your usual caution in making any judgements?" asked Watson.

There was a pause before Holmes began to explain.

"This room is the same size as the ones we have been offered, is it not?" said Holmes.

Watson nodded that he believed they were but with such a look that cued Holmes to continue.

"Do you notice any difference between your room and this one?" Sherlock asked.

Watson studied the four walls of the room, then looked at the floor and examined the glittering ceiling, inevitably drawn to the spectacular chandeliers, then looked out of the window, clearly still unsure of Holmes' insinuation.

"Is it something to do with the furniture?"

"Warmer," said Holmes.

"Is it that impressive chest of drawers?"

Holmes said nothing.

"Is it this gigantic bed?" said Watson.

"Warmer!" conveyed Sherlock.

"It's a very nice bed," said Watson examining it from top to bottom. "It's a big bed."

"Warmer!" proclaimed Holmes.

Watson looked perplexed but continued his examination as if he were assessing a medical patient's anatomy.

"Ok, just tell me, Holmes. What are you thinking?"

"How many pillows does the bed have?"

"Three," answered Watson.

"My room has the same size bed, no doubt yours does, too. How many pillows are there you on bed, Watson?"

"Ah, I see. There must be at least four on our beds. Yes, three pillows wouldn't go with this size bed. So, Holmes you are surmising that a pillow has been removed, probably by the perpetrator?" "Quite possibly."

The two then discussed why anyone, but especially the perpetrator, would remove a pillow from the room. The obvious answer was that the pillow had important clues about the crime, and maybe even the criminal.

"So, it's possible, if not likely, that the criminal removed the pillow clue but made no apparent attempt to remove the poisoning clues," opined Watson. "I wonder why he or she would do that?"

"I would have thought that answer was obvious," said Holmes.

Holmes and Watson then discussed what possible clues might be on the pillow. Blood, signs of a struggle like a rip in the cover, saliva, tears, fingernail fragments, poison, were all possible clues.

"Well, if we are correct, Watson, this almost certainly rules out any likelihood of suicide or even an accident," said Sherlock. "We are indeed looking at a murder scene."

The two investigators continued their examination separately, searching for any clues.

After a while, Sherlock asked his friend to help him dismantle the bed before he made his way down to the lab to fully inspect Nat's corpse. Holmes was looking for further clues. Often key clues were hidden or merely out of sight and Sherlock wanted to ensure there wasn't anything under the bed, or hidden within the frame, that could contain valuable information.

The two of them removed the sheets and then attempted to lift the enormous mattress. The mattress was heavy, and between them, after considerable effort, the two investigators eventually managed to remove it from the bedframe.

"What's this?" said Watson.

The pair looked down and saw a large envelope that had been under the mattress but now sat atop the bedframe.

Sherlock picked up the sealed padded envelope and examined it. Carefully, he opened it.

"Good Lord!" said Watson.

Holmes pulled out the contents of the envelope, about five thousand pounds in large bank notes that had been hidden under the bed.

"Why would Nat have this much money under his bed?" asked Watson.

"Did the perpetrator even know about the money? And if so, why did he leave it there. Or," continued Holmes, "perhaps he planted it there?"

"Seems unlikely, but clearly the money is now a factor in this case," said Watson.

They had just finished putting the bed back together when there was a knock on the door.

"Can I have a few words with you gentlemen, please?" asked Ron.

Chapter Seven

Tuesday 6:30pm

"Definition, rationality, and structure are ways of seeing, but they become prisons when they blank out other ways of seeing."
A. R. Ammons

"Sherlock, why don't you start interviewing the suspects? I'm going to study Nat's body," said Watson after their meeting with Ron.

"Don't you mean persons of interest?" responded Holmes.

"Okay, if you're going to so bloody picky and Americanized, 'persons of interest'," chirped Watson in reply.

"I'm not being picky, but you know as well as I do that a suspect is someone where there is evidence to suggest they committed the crime, whereas a person of interest is someone who might have valuable information about the crime. There's a difference," Holmes strongly demanded. "You know what they say about assumptions, Watson."

"Okay. You're right as usual. Fancy that? What is the phrase about assumptions? Assume: to pull an emu out of your ass, or something like that. I will go and examine Nat and you can interview those persons of interest," he said emphasizing the last three words.

And with that, Watson left for the lab in the basement where Nat's body was being kept and Holmes headed to Shane's office.

"Dr. Kenwight, can I speak with you now?" Holmes asked as Shane opened the door to a rather grand ground floor office.

Shane hesitated briefly before agreeing. He then offered Sherlock a seat as Holmes pulled out a tape recorder.

"I hope you don't mind," said Holmes "but it helps me focus on the conversation and not spend my time taking notes."

Shane nodded his assent while silently revisiting Holmes' apparent rejection of modern technology. A tape recorder?

"Where do we begin?" asked the doctor.

"We don't know much about any of you, so we just want to get a few details about your life and your relationships with the team and, of course, Nat," said Watson. "Once MI6 get involved, they'll do much more extensive questioning."

"Where should I begin?" asked Shane.

"Please tell me about your life. What led to you being here at this moment of time?" said Holmes.

"I grew up in Oxford. Both my parents were doctors. I had two younger sisters and an adopted brother. We moved to St. Albans when I was ten."

"How was family life at that time?" asked Watson.

"We were all pretty nerdy. A lot of the time we all sat around reading our own books. We were all fairly smart, but the house wasn't well-maintained and for the most part the emphasis was on intellectual pursuits rather than experiences. We hardly ever went on vacations and whenever we did it seemed like we spent all our time in museums rather than the beach or at the fair."

"Did you have many friends, growing up?"

"Yes, I did. There were a few classmates in elementary school who were interested in the same sort of things that I was. We played board games and made model airplanes and boats and even once created some fireworks."

"Was religion or spirituality part of your upbringing?"

"We didn't really participate in it, but we talked a lot about it. That was typical of who we were, a lot of thinking and talking but not much doing."

"Did you follow a particular religion?"

"We were Protestants. We rarely went to church except maybe on Easter or Christmas. We didn't even celebrate Christmas much. We rarely had a tree, although as kids we did get some presents."

"Do you believe there's a heaven?" asked Holmes.

Shane looked quizzically at the investigator before asking the point of the question.

"I have my reasons," said Holmes unhelpfully but implying he wanted Shane to reply.

"No, I don't actually believe in heaven. I understand the limits of human comprehension and that anything is theoretically a possibility, but I just don't have the faith and it is faith that is needed to believe in many of these religious and spiritual concepts," said Shane.

"Thank you for answering that. Okay, please tell me about your college experiences?"

"I really got involved at University College, Oxford. I joined the boat club and enjoyed rowing. I was the coxswain and reveled in being a little eccentric and taking risky routes. I also got into classical music and science fiction."

"What about your personal life?" asked Watson.

"I fell in love with a graduate student who was just a few years younger than me. Her name was Janet. Initially, she continued her studies for her doctorate in London while I was in Oxford. We were married for fifteen years and had two children."

Holmes then asked Dr. Kenwight whether he had ever been involved in a case like this. The doctor answered that he never had been this close to such a crime. He mentioned that he had a colleague in his early days as a professor who died under mysterious circumstances while vacationing in South America but apart from that, nothing had ever been this close to home.

"Well, thank you for that background. Now the next question obviously is, what possible reason could anyone have for murdering Nat?" said Holmes.

"I've been pondering that myself," said Shane. "I am really having trouble coming up with an idea let alone an answer. If it was a murder, I can only assume that somehow the Chinese got to him. But I just don't see how that is possible. To be honest, I can imagine a suicide more than I can a murder."

"Why do you say that?"

"Nat could be very self-effacing. He could always find ways in which he thought he could do better. Of course, that drove him to incredible achievements, but his self-deprecation could get very low. I noted some signs of sadness yesterday, too."

"Did he ever talk of killing himself?"

Shane shook his head. "I don't think it ever got that bad."

"What was your relationship with him like?" asked Holmes.

Shane shifted a little uncomfortably in his chair. "He could be difficult but for the most part I admired his genius," admitted the doctor.

"How did he come to be working here at Bletchley?"

Shane explained how he was invited by MI6 to be part of a special team of experts to recruit the best and most appropriate talent to form the group. Nat's name was on a short list for the AI specialist role.

"I knew about his work, of course, and I had heard him talk, but I had never met him. His credentials were unmatched, so it seemed a relatively easy decision. However, I was concerned about his disposition. I didn't want his negativity to impact the rest of the group."

"What do you mean, Dr. Kenwight?"

Shane paused for a moment and stared long and awkwardly down at the floor.

Sherlock waited until Shane looked up and continued.

"Mr. Holmes, Janet was a lovely young lady when we married. She was delightful. Except she had one problem. She could be extremely negative. It got worse over time, to the point where I simply couldn't take it any longer."

Shane stopped as he became emotional. Holmes knew to say nothing and wait. Eventually, the doctor continued.

"I tried to get her help. We went to counselling. She was very reticent about taking medication, and that drove me insane. It was an awful roller-coaster. That's why I divorced her."

Shane stopped again. And once more, Holmes waited patiently.

Eventually, Shane ejected the sputum of emotion that had been building up inside.

"She killed herself ten months later."

"Oh my God!" said Holmes.

"Yes. I was so badly hurt. I felt it was my fault. But then I was also angry at her for rejecting treatment that could have helped her and for damaging our kids' lives."

"You have two children, right?"

"Yes. A boy and a girl. They're grown now and doing okay," said Shane wistfully.

Holmes waited until the cloud of emotion enveloping Shane dissipated before continuing.

"So, you are naturally very sensitive to anyone with a negative disposition, is that what you are saying?" asked Holmes for clarification.

"I guess so. I had never articulated it quite that way, but I think I am. If I had observed that about Nat in my interviews with him and my research on him, I might not have recommended him. But on the other hand, he was brilliant, and his recent activity might well have turned the war," said Shane.

"So, you were part of the team that selected all of the leaders here today?" asked Holmes.

"Yes. For the most part the selections were unanimous. I didn't have a say in the selection of the government liaison officer, Ron McFerie, but everyone else, yes, I did. I had some doubts initially about Rue, the administration chief, but she has been an absolute blessing."

"What were you concerns about her?"
"I'm not completely sure, to be honest. I think I just wondered whether she was experienced enough. But fortunately, I have been proven wrong. She is incredibly focused."

Sherlock asked for further clarification.

"Rue is able to focus her attention exceptionally well. In fact, being on and attentive seems like her default position." Shane hesitated for second before continuing to underscore the point he was making.

"I don't want to blind you with science, Mr. Holmes, but let me give you a brief explanation so you can better understand what I mean about Rue," Shane continued.

"In the brain there is something called The Default Mode Network. This is the state of unfocussed thinking, even creativity. You're not processing thoughts, you are more experiencing things without too much, or any, judgement." Shane stopped to ensure that Holmes was following along.

"Now there's another part of the brain, The Frontal Parietal Network, that is used when processing and focusing. The brain waves are higher in that state, suggesting significant activity. The issue is, how do people switch from one system to the other, in either direction from the Default Mode Network to the Frontal Parietal Network or in the reverse direction? You follow me so far?"

Holmes nodded and Shane continued.

"There's a third network called The Salience Network, and this determines what is important at any one time and switches to the Frontal Parietal Network when we need to focus, and out of that to the Default Mode Network when there is no need for cognitive processing and focus."

"So would people who have attention deficit disorder have a difficult time switching to the frontal network to focus?" asked Holmes.

"Yes, exactly. And so would those with obsessive-compulsive disorder. Now here's the point. Rue shows the opposite tendency. She seems to be almost always in the Frontal Parietal region, in a state of extreme focus," said Shane. "That's incredibly valuable, especially for a chief admin officer who has many things to track, record, and process."

With his lesson in neuroscience over, Sherlock resumed the conversation.

"What's your perception of the other team members and their relationship with Nat?" asked Sherlock.

"I think they all got on pretty well with him, as much as he allowed. He would often isolate himself. Ron can get a little peeved that amongst the scientists he doesn't get the credit he deserves. I think he gets frustrated with all the talk about robots and artificial intelligence. He also seems to have gotten a little more ornery lately. Probably all the pressure of this damned conflict. He is the one who has to deal with the military bureaucracy, and I know for sure that isn't fun."

"Last night, who else was on the property?"

"Well, in this building, just the seven of us, and Sandra in housekeeping and the two night security guards. As far as I know, there were no reports of anything unusual last night. It is rare for anyone else to come here to the Range unless specifically invited, especially at night. They have to ask permission, and even when they do it's rarely given unless it's a total emergency. I want to give the team some space to relax in the evening. It's a very stressful job."

Holmes asked who else did occasionally come on the property.

"We have a permanent guard on duty at the gate, Lee during the day and Todd at night, but they rarely, if ever, come to this building. And they themselves are very strict about enforcing rules and not letting anyone in if they don't already have clearance. Then, separately, there's the two daytime and two nighttime security guards. We have Sandra and Allison, daytime and nighttime receptionists who take care of the housekeeping, prepare meals, do the laundry, that sort of thing. We have a general manager, Matt, who takes care of the grounds, and anything needed inside the building, and that's about it. We have a specialized cleaning service run by a woman called Marissa who come once a week and groundkeepers who also come on a weekly basis. Dennis and his crew come once a year to fix up the furniture, and Brian and Paula sometimes come in to make a special dinner. Steve and Bonnie come in every year to fix any flooring issues, but for the most part, we try to keep this place as secluded and secure as possible," said Shane.

"What about contact with people outside the Range?" asked Holmes.

"We mostly stay here. Occasionally, Mary and Rue will go to a gym they like, even though we do have some equipment here. The people at the gym are reliable and have all been checked. Frank, Adam, Trevor, Maureen and Cherie. Once in a blue moon Earl will go fishing with a guy called Tommy, and Rob play a round of golf with his friend Chris, but that's about it. There's really no time for these pleasures."

"If you like, I can arrange for you to talk with the two night guards," Shane added.

"That would be perfect," Holmes replied.

"In the meantime, why don't you and Watson join me for dinner. I'll ask Ron to come as well. You'll definitely want to speak with him as soon as possible. Let me see if he is available," Shane said, picking up his phone.

While Holmes waited patiently, he perused Shane's office. There were photos of his children and even of his deceased wife, as well as many diplomas and certificates from numerous esteemed academic institutions.

"That's odd," said Shane putting down his phone. "I can't seem to get hold of Ron." That's when he saw the text from Rue.

Ron has gone off property. Left a few minutes ago. Didn't say where he was going. Said he told you he was leaving. WTF?

Shane looked perplexed and repeated the phrase 'WTF' out loud. "WTF?" asked Holmes inquisitively. Before Shane had a chance to answer, Sherlock had worked out the meaning.

"Oh, I see," said Holmes. "WTF means Watson's Theoretical Foundation. When I was teaching my colleague about investigative science, we started to focus on his core beliefs, which formed the theoretical foundation for his perception and reasoning. It's important to know your implicit biases, you know. I remember that now: WTF."

"Well, whatever, but that is not what Rue wanted to convey. Ron has simply left the building," said Shane in annoyance.

"Is that a common occurrence?" asked Holmes.

"No. In fact, anyone leaving the property has to inform me first," said Shane angrily.

Holmes suggested that perhaps Ron had to respond to a family emergency.

"Ron doesn't really have a family. He has two grown children who are very independent. And one of them lives in the United States. I have no idea why he left. This is very concerning."

"Are any of the other team members married?" asked Sherlock.

Shane informed Holmes that none of the main team were currently married. This was a deliberate decision by the government authorities to recruit unattached experts, so they would not be distracted from their core duties.

While Sherlock understood the logic, he briefly wondered whether, and how, their collective single status might affect the dynamics of the team and the behavior of its members.

While Holmes was musing on the notion, and possible implication of seven unmarried experts, basically locked in the same location for months at a time, Shane was clearly upset about Ron's sudden and forbidden departure.

"Should we notify the police about Ron?" asked Shane.

Holmes didn't seem too concerned.

"Yes, you can do that if you wish, but personally I would not want to involve the police in this matter. I think there's probably a very good reason for his departure and I wouldn't be surprised if he returns shortly. However, I do recommend you call your superiors at MI6 immediately and tell them."

Shane agreed that was a better course of action and arranged to call his superiors at MI6 immediately. Before doing so, he reminded Sherlock that the security night shift had arrived outside. He knew that Holmes wanted to talk to them immediately, before anyone else had a chance to influence their perceptions.

"They're right outside the building. I'll tell them you're coming now," said Shane.

"No, don't do that. I'll find them, I'm sure."

"Okay. It's Dave and Khang."

"Sorry, what was the second name?" asked Holmes.

"Khang: K. H. A. N. G." replied Shane.

Holmes paused for a moment.

"That's a Chinese name, right?"

Shane nodded in the affirmative.

"If you don't mind me asking, why on earth, when we are at war with the Chinese, would you employ a Chinese person, as a security officer no less?"

"Rest assured, Sherlock, Khang is a great man and very patriotic towards the United Kingdom, his country of birth. In fact, he has been quite helpful to us when it comes to understanding traditional Chinese thinking. You'll enjoy talking with him."

Sherlock expressed his ambivalence and headed out to interview the night security team.

Chapter Eight

Tuesday 7:15pm

*"True intuitive expertise is learned from prolonged
experience with good feedback on mistakes."*
Daniel Kahneman

On his way out of the building, Sherlock called Watson and asked him how he was progressing with his analysis of Nat's body.

"Well, I'd put the time of death between midnight and two in the morning. Definite signs of poisoning but still not entirely sure that was the sole reason for his death. There might also have been some respiratory issues, too. Other than that, I'm finished here for the moment."

When Watson told him he had just finished, Sherlock suggested he join him outside to talk to the nighttime security guards.

It didn't take him long to locate Dave and Khang, the two night security guards. He introduced himself to them and started to address the security protocols.

Dave, a tall physically strong man with dark curly hair, explained that most of the surveillance was geared to the exterior of the building. There were cameras in the lobby of the main floor of the accommodations building, but nowhere else inside.

"We have checked that video from last night and there appears to be nothing unusual at all," said Khang. "Just Sandra, the nighttime receptionist, wandering around the lobby, cleaning things up, as she always does. No-one else in the video."

At that moment Watson arrived and was introduced to the two guards.

Khang then explained that he and Dave spent most of their time on duty outside the building, watching for any unusual activity.

"It was very quiet last night as it is most nights. Anyone who works here knows that they have to get clearance before coming here after work hours," said Dave. "And that rarely happens."

"If someone were to get into the building without alerting either of you, how would they do that?" asked Watson.

The two guards looked at each other as they considered the question.

"Probably they would try to distract us, and while we were distracted, try to sneak in through the back door. But even then, the back door is locked, and an alarm goes off if it is opened. Honestly, we have never faced that situation," said Dave. "We did check it a few minutes ago and there's no sign of any activity, forced entry or anything like that."

"Could they not break a window or enter another way?" continued Watson.

"Unlikely, Mr. Watson. There are alarms on the windows, too," said Khang.

"Who has access to the room where those alarms can be deactivated?" asked Holmes.

"Just the two of us, and Dr. Kenwight, I believe. It might be possible that some of the others have access, too, but we don't know that."
"Can you show us that room, please?" said Holmes.

The two guards looked at each other for assurance.

"Sir, we did check it a while ago and everything seemed in place. There was nothing suspicious there at all," said Dave.

"I would like to see it nonetheless," insisted Holmes.

Dave led the investigators to a hidden stairway that went down to a room in the basement, while Khang stayed on duty outside.

Dave unlocked the door and led them into the small room that hosted a massive spider web of interconnected cables.

"Has this system ever been deactivated?" asked Holmes.

"We do a check once a year where we turn it off and back on to make sure it's all working," said Dave.

When asked by Watson, Dave told them that the system had only ever been switched on and off at the source by unplugging various interconnections.

"Could the system be accessed virtually from the outside?" queried Watson.

"I don't believe it has ever been accessed that way. There are inbuilt precautions against it," said the security guard.

Holmes snooped around the room for a few minutes before asking Dave another question.

"How do you get along with Khang?"

"We get along fine, sir. He's a great bloke. If you're suggesting that he might be a risk because of his Chinese heritage, Mr. Holmes, you are heading down the completely wrong path. We agree on everything. Oh, except he is an Arsenal fan and I support Spurs. He's a Brit through and through."

Holmes thanked him for his opinion.

"One last thing before we head upstairs, Dave. Who do you think did this dastardly act?"

"I think that's for you to figure out, sir. It's a total mystery to me. I'm inclined to think that Nat killed himself. I can't imagine who else would do it," answered Dave.

"Well, if you had to choose your most likely suspect, who would it be?"

"I don't think I can say, sir," said Dave before he was interrupted by Holmes.

"This is just between us. It'll never go anywhere else. Please trust me on this."

Dave squinted off into the distance as he was thinking how to reply.

"Well, sir," Dave started very hesitantly, "If I had to choose one of them, I would guess it would be…" He stopped and shook his head, "No, I can't believe any of them did it."

Sherlock encouraged the security guard to guess, reassuring him that he wouldn't give any value on his choice of suspect.

"Well, if I had to choose one of them, I would guess it was," he paused again. "It was Ron," he blurted out.

"Why do you say that?" asked Holmes.

"Simply because Mr. Ron can be a bit grouchy at times. That's all. He seems to have been a little more irritable in recent weeks."

Holmes thanked Dave for his guess and reassured him that it would remain private.

"Oh, by the way, did you see Ron leaving the campus today?" asked Holmes.

"Has he left? We didn't check or feel the need to. We've been inspecting the grounds and building as I have explained, since we arrived." Dave checked his phone. "There's no official record of him leaving."

Holmes waved his hands as if to indicate that was the end of that particular subject and the three of them left the security room and headed up to meet up with Khang.

When they got outside, Khang met them and reassured them that nothing of any significance had happened since they had been down in the security basement. At that point Sherlock asked Khang whether he and Watson could have a few words with him. Dave acknowledged that he would stand guard while Khang left for a conversation with the investigators.

Holmes led Watson and Khang into the outer part of the garden and to the edge of the lake, beyond hearing distance from the main building and Dave.

"What do you make of this whole saga, Khang?" asked Holmes.

"It's a total mystery, Mr. Holmes. I have no idea who could have done this," Khang said, shaking his head.

"If you were to make one guess, who would be your likeliest candidate?"

"I have no idea. They all seem to get on so well together. Really, I don't have a clue."

"Well, you never know, you might have a clue and not know it," suggested Holmes.

Khang smiled and shrugged his shoulders.

"I know this seems like an unreasonable question and we promise you whatever you say on this will be kept secret. Just take a guess," added Watson.

"Well, if I had to pick anyone it would be Ron, but I really don't imagine he would actually do it."

Sherlock asked why Khang chose Ron.

"We've seen him get angry a few times, that's all, especially lately. All the others seem to care for each other so much, it's inconceivable that it was any of the others," said Khang.

Sherlock thanked him for his answer and again reassured him that the conversation would remain private.

"One last thing," said Holmes. "How do you and Dave get on?" Khang didn't miss a beat.

"Dave is a great bloke. I love working with him. Except for one thing," said Khang.

Both Holmes and Watson sent him an enquiring look.

"He's a Spurs fan," said Khang, breaking into a loud laugh.

"That's interesting," said Watson. "Will he be going to the American Football game that's being played at the Tottenham Hotspur stadium this Sunday? It's the Jacksonville Jaguars against the Dallas Cowboys."

"You'll have to ask him that," said Khang before asking Watson, "So, you're interested in American Football?"

"Yes, I enjoy it but mostly because I like to wager on it," said Watson. "A harmless gamble makes the game a bit more interesting. And I also have access to a prediction company that is pretty good at beating the odds."

"That's very interesting. Does this company get the results right most of the time?" asked Khang.

There was a pause.

"Khang, what percentage of points played does a leading tennis professional win against his main opponents?" asked Watson.

Both Holmes and the security officer looked quizzically at Watson. Khang seemed to be thinking the question over. After a brief pause, he gave his answer.

"About 75% of the points played?" suggested Khang

"No. It's actually about 54%," said Watson much to the surprise of the security guard.

"It's really that low?" asked Khang.

Watson nodded in the affirmative. "Yes, the difference between success and mediocrity is relatively small."

"You've lost me there," said Khang. "What's that have to do with predicting sports, like Yankee football?"

"Intuality, the prediction analytics company, has a great track record predicting sports, and a lot of other things. They're right about 58% of the time in sports, which is very high and beats pretty much everyone else. And 58% will ensure great returns on wagers," said Watson.

"Okay, well enough of that, we have a lot of work to do," said Holmes, getting irritated by Watson's distraction.

And with that, Holmes and Watson thanked Khang for his time and headed back into the building.

The two investigators entered Holmes' room and ensured the door was shut.

"Oh, before I forget," Holmes started, "When Rue sent Shane a message about Ron's 'disappearance' she said 'WTF.' I pretended I didn't know that meant "what the fuck" and suggested WTF referred to Watson's Theoretical Foundation, a part of your training. So. if they ask you about that, please remember that WTF means Watson's Theoretical Foundation."

Watson laughed out loud.

"They must think you are totally ignorant about the internet, social media and anything related to computers."

"Well, that's the idea," said Holmes. Then he continued.

"Have you heard from Ron?"

"Yes," said Watson. "He texted a while ago to say that he had arrived."

"Very good," said Holmes.

Chapter Nine

Tuesday 7:45pm

"Beware of false knowledge. It is more dangerous than ignorance."
George Bernard Shaw

The two detectives shared their latest updates. Holmes was particularly interested in what Watson had found during his assessment of Nat's body.

"It's more complicated than I thought," said Watson. "There's definitely some poison in his system. I believe it to be strychnine."

"Ah, rat poison," said Holmes, referring to the fact that strychnine is sometimes used as a rodent killer.

The two almost simultaneously mused about whether the pest control service Natural Exterminators used strychnine in their attempts to keep the grounds and the residence itself, free of pests. They would have to wait until tomorrow to find out.

"Was there anything else?" asked Holmes.

Watson assured his colleague that he was confident that the strychnine was the likely cause of death.

The two pondered as to whether this could perhaps be an unfortunate accident. Even if strychnine was used, how would Nat intake enough to kill him? Did the exterminators spray or place an inappropriate amount of the poison in Nat's room? Did it somehow contaminate some food that Nat might have had sitting on the table?

Holmes had searched the room and didn't find any evidence of food or crumbs that suggested that Nat had recently eaten. The mini refrigerator contained some cheese and beer, and the cabinet above it had a bag of unopened apples, but that was all the food there was.

"I studied his teeth, mouth, hands and nails, and there was nothing there to suggest he had recently eaten," said Watson.

"And, of course, there's the mystery of the missing pillow," added Holmes.

"Let's go and question Sandra, the night housekeeper, and then make a list of questions we need to ask the others. Hopefully, we'll be able to talk to some of them this evening."

They headed downstairs and found Sandra sitting at her desk in the reception area. Sandra had her dark hair rolled up in a bun, a modest amount of makeup, and red reading glasses that matched her sweater. She looked up at the two detectives as they approached her.

"My dear, may we please ask you some questions?" said Holmes as he approached her desk.

Sandra, of course, knew about these two blokes and was expecting them to question her. Not that she felt she had anything of value to offer. Last night had been just another quiet evening, like every other evening. Nothing unusual had happened at all. Just as boring as ever.

"I don't think I have anything useful to say, but please, ask away," she said as Holmes directed her into her office and shut the door. "Honestly, sir, it was just another boring night. Nothing at all. No one called for nothing. I didn't hear no unusual noises. I just did what I did what I always do – tidy up, clean the place, make sure everything was ready for the morning – you know, put out the tea, coffee and cups, that sorta thing," she said in a distinct Cockney accent.

"Would you have heard anyone leaving or going into or out of a room?" asked Sherlock.

"It really depends on how noisy they were, to be honest. I would hear a door slamming shut, or someone knocking on a door, but if they were real quiet, chances are I wouldn't notice it."

"How common is it for people to call down to you to ask for something during the evening?" Holmes asked.

"Honestly, not very much. Occasionally one of 'em might call for a bottle of water, something like that, but once they go to their rooms for the night, it's pretty quiet."

"Does anyone call down about cleaning or laundry, or stuff like that?" asked Watson.

"No, they all know to put any laundry they want done in the laundry room, and they're good about doing that."

"So, is that just for their clothes, or do they put other things there, like the pillowcases and bed sheets?"

"No, the cleaning staff change the linens about once a week. I suppose if someone wanted something like a cushion or pillowcase cleaned, they would simply take it to the laundry room."

Watson asked Sandra what was currently in the laundry room and whether she knew what had been placed when and by whom.

"I can take you there and we can have a look, if you'd like," said Sandra.

Before they left to investigate the laundry, Holmes confirmed with Sandra that the cleaners had not been in Nat's room since yesterday morning and had been prevented from entering it today.

"One last thing before we leave, Miss Sandra," said Sherlock. "What do you make of this mystery?"

"Beats me," said the housekeeper. "I have no idea what happened. I'm as shocked as everyone else is."

"What was your relationship with Nat like?"

"He was a pleasant enough bloke. Pretty quiet and a bit nerdy, like the rest of them."

And with that, the three headed out to the laundry room.

When they reached the laundry room, the dryers were going.

"Usually, they just put the things to wash here on this counter-top, but it looks like the housekeeping girls have washed what was here today. It'll be my job to empty the dryers when they're done and fold the clothes. You wanna see what's washing?" asked Sandra.

Watson and Holmes nodded with an unusual certainty.

Sandra stopped the dryers and open the doors.

"Looks like today was sheets and pillowcases day," Sandra said as she stepped back from the machines.

Holmes and Watson exchanged glances before Sherlock spoke.

"So, all the pillowcases were washed today?"

"All except Dr. Nat's, yes," responded Sandra.

Watson asked how many pillowcases that should be.

Sandra quickly did the math.

"Normally it would be seven times the four pillowcases, which makes, er...er...er...er...er... twenty-six, right?"

Watson corrected her arithmetic. "No, that's twenty-eight."

"Oh. Sorry about that. Never was much good at math," said Sandra rather forlornly. Then she continued.

"So, twenty-eight minus the four in Dr. Nat's room would make, er...er....twenty-four?"

She looked inquisitively at Watson hoping her math was correct this time.

"That is correct, Miss Sandra," Watson said with a smile as Holmes cringed silently. Then Sherlock spoke, wishing to move on with the evening's schedule.

"Well, Sandra, when these have finished drying...what's that, about twenty minutes... could you separate the pillowcases from the remainder of the wash and leave them on the counter there so we can examine them?"

"What have pillowcases got to do with your investigation?" asked Sandra.

"Well, probably nothing, my dear, but we would like to inspect them," said Holmes. "Okay, lets head back to your office so you can get on with your evening's work."

As they left the laundry area Holmes had another question.

"Do you know who collected the laundry this morning?"

"That would be Allison. She's the daytime receptionist. She'll be here around nine tomorrow morning if you would like to talk to her," responded Sandra.

Sherlock expressed his gratitude about the information.

"You don't have to say anything to her, Sandra. We would rather you didn't. We'll catch up with Allison in the morning. And we'll see you in a little while in the laundry room," added Holmes as he and Watson stepped away from Sandra's office.

Chapter Ten

Tuesday 8:00pm

"We don't see very far in the future, we are very focused on one idea at a time, one problem at a time, and all these are incompatible with rationality as economic theory assumes it."
Daniel Kahneman

Holmes and Watson returned to Shane's office, where the director was still quite worried about Ron's leaving.

"I can't understand why Ron left without telling anyone. Surely this makes him the major suspect?" said Shane.

"While it looks suspicious, we have to be very careful about jumping to conclusions before we have any more information. I am sure you're aware of one of the cognitive biases – the anchoring bias, Dr. Kenwight. If you focus on one theory this early in the investigation it tends to influence all subsequent perceptions, and we can't allow that to happen."

"There are several cognitive biases, are there not?" asked Shane.

Watson explained that there were more than a hundred and fifty that had been recognized currently. Kenwight wanted to know more, so Watson delved a little deeper.

"Human beings aren't logical; they are psychological, often with the emphasis on the psycho."

Shane smiled in agreement.

"That's one of my favorite quotes about humanity," added Sherlock before nodding to Watson to continue.

"Now it should be noted that while many of these thinking patterns are called biases, there are also effective cognitive strategies. For example, looking for confirmation of any perception or theory is an important cognitive strategy. Because of that, it can become "overused" and become more influential than perhaps is warranted," said Watson.

"I am guessing that some of these "biases" are more important than others?" asked Shane.

"Yes, indeed," Holmes acknowledged.

"The Confirmation and Anchoring Bias are very common. And so is the Availability bias, which is critical in our line of work. The Availability bias refers to the fact that we are much more influenced by what information is available. For example, if you arrive at a crime scene and there is the distinct smell of alcohol, there is a tendency to start framing your ideas based around alcohol consumption but that might be an irrelevant cue. We have to constantly be aware of the exformation - the information that is excluded for one reason or another – not just the information that is right in front of us," added Holmes.

"So, while Ron's disappearance might seem suspicious, we need to be careful on not over interpreting his absence. What are the other key biases?" asked Shane.

The investigators continued highlighting the key cognitive biases. "Quality and quantity bias are also key in objectively assessing data, as I am sure you're well aware as a scientist and researcher, Dr. Kenwight," said Holmes.

"Absolutely," acknowledged Shane. "Some qualitative data is irrelevant if it is derived from just a few examples. And some quantitative data lacks any quality. I totally understand it."

Watson then continued by addressing the issue of risk and risk averseness.

"We know generally that people are risk averse up to a certain point. However, once the probability of a greater return increases, people are generally prepared to bite the bullet," added Watson.

"What's the ratio that's the tipping point?" asked Shane.

"Research shows it's about 2.5 to 1. In other words, if the return on taking the risk exceeds 2.5 to 1, people are much more prepared to take the risk. So, for example, if I said you could gamble ten pounds with the chance of winning ten pounds you wouldn't find that terribly appealing. But if I said, you could bet ten pounds with a chance of winning thirty quid, you would find that much more tempting," said Watson.

"What other important biases are there?" asked Shane.

"One I think that is very important is memory decay," said Holmes. "Computers, like humans, often keep their data for way too long, long after it has lost its utility, especially in prediction. It drives me bonkers, for example when I hear a soccer announcer spout off a lot of statistics about a team going back ten, twenty, or more years! What happened that long ago has no relevance to today and certainly has no predictive value. We need to practice memory decay in that once data has lost its relevance, we should forget about it."

"What's that called -- memory decay? It's an excellent point. That sometimes applies to science, too, especially studies about people from a totally different era and culture. How white middle-class people reacted to an experiment fifty years ago may be quite irrelevant today even to the same class of people, let alone totally different ethnic and socio-economic groups," confirmed Dr. Kenwight.

"Well, that raises another critical bias. The symmetry bias," said Watson. "We are programmed to seek patterns in things, but this can often go too far. It's one of the key lessons that Sherlock has taught me – don't be too enamored by your perception of patterns and similarity."

"To be honest," interjected Sherlock, "this is one of my biggest concerns with artificial intelligence. Sure, it's wonderful to be able to mine historical data, but the question is, how relevant is it? That's where appreciation of context is key and is part of what human intelligence has to offer. Similarity does not mean causality, or even meaningful association."

Holmes continued. "Are you aware of the high correlation of the number of people who died by getting entangled in their bedsheets and per capita cheese consumption? Or the almost perfect correlation between the divorce rate in Maine and per capita margarine consumption? And one that particularly fascinates me is the very strong relationship between the age of Miss America and the number of murders by steam, hot vapors and hot objects?"

"All of this is studied by Tyler Vigen, which he publishes on his Spurious Correlations website," Holmes said.

Shane smiled at the examples Holmes stated and commented that even in science, particularly in science, one has to be very cautious about interpreting apparent symmetry and patterns.

At this point Shane interrupted Holmes and suggested that this information would be very valuably shared with the rest of the team.

"I'm sure some of the team know about these biases but maybe not in such depth. Would you be willing to continue this discussion with the rest of the team if I could get them together right now?"

"Yes. We just have to talk to Sandra about something and then we will come down to the conference room," said Holmes.

Chapter Eleven

Tuesday: 8:30pm

"Cognitive psychology tells us that the unaided human mind is vulnerable to many fallacies and illusions because of its reliance on its memory for vivid anecdotes rather than systematic statistics."
Steven Pinker

Sandra arrived to tell the investigators that the washing cycle was complete.

When they reached the laundry room Sandra showed them that what she had done with the laundry.

"I've separately laid out the pillowcases as you asked me to do," said Sandra pointing to the linens lying on a nearby table as they reached the laundry room.

"How many pillowcases are there?" asked Holmes.

"Oh, sir, I didn't count. I thought there were 24," said Sandra.

Holmes and Sandra watched as Watson laid the pillows out in stacks of four. There were 24 pillows.

"Hmm, that doesn't tell us much," opined Watson as the two investigators began a study of each pillow.

They both understood that just because there were 24 pillowcases, that did not mean that the crime scene pillowcase was not amongst them. The perpetrator could easily have replaced a "normal" pillowcase with one used in the crime.

"Ah, look at this," said Sherlock holding up one of the pillowcases. Holmes was investigating what appeared to be a small tear at the top of one of the pillowcases. It was about half an inch in length.

The investigators speculated on why such a tear might occur. Perhaps it was a result of struggle?

"These things don't tear very easily," suggested Sandra.

On continuing their inspection, the two investigators also found a smaller tear on the other side of the pillowcase.

"Is there any way of knowing whose pillowcase this was?" asked Watson, "Or at least who put it in the laundry pile?"

Sandra nodded her head from side to side before suggesting, rather unconvincingly, that Allison might know.

The conversation was over and Holmes and Watson headed to the conference room.

Shane had explained to the assembled team that Holmes and Watson had been talking about cognitive biases and he thought that they would benefit from hearing this impromptu presentation.

"We have explained cognitive biases that most of you probably know," said Holmes.

"There's confirmation bias, the tendency to only seek information that confirms what you want to believe. Then there's the availability bias in which you are overly influenced by the information that is available and the anchoring bias, where initial thoughts can fashion the entire decision process," said Holmes.

Rue commented that she was very aware of the symmetry bias, where we constantly look for, and create patterns, that don't exist.

"And talking of symmetry and pattern seeking, another bias is called 'the hot hand fallacy,' which refers to the rather irrational belief that someone on a hot streak, perhaps winning several hands at a card game, will keep doing so. Logic implies that someone on a hot streak is soon going to lose because a hot hand can't continue forever," added Watson.

"Does the environment bias our thinking?" asked Shane.

"Of course," said Holmes. "We totally underestimate how the physical and even social environment influences our minds and our bodies."

The comment made Shane wonder about how the dynamics of the team and indeed the whole operation might now change with Nat out of the picture. He assumed that in due course someone else would be appointed to replace Nat, but that, too, would almost certainly alter the team dynamics. He reflected on how good the team chemistry had actually been and made a mental note that Nat's successor must be chosen on his ability to enhance the team.

At this point Watson interjected with an important part of the puzzle.

"Folks, I don't mean to be offensive here, but many people, even those working with artificial intelligence, don't understand the full scale of human information processing. Humans have trillions of cells in their bodies and brains that are in constant complex connection. Under our skin and our skulls, 11 million bits of information are being processed per second. These incredible multi-cellular connections are the infrastructure of our functioning, even our thoughts. We are not conscious of this system because such awareness would be overwhelming and absorb all our energy."

The team listened intently as Sherlock let his medical colleague expand more on the amazing mind-body complex.

"There have been several books that explore this incredible system that makes us who we are," continued Watson. "For example, Candace Pert's book *Molecules of Emotion* explains how emotions are not just psychological experiences but are also physical, and how they can affect our health and wellbeing. Pert describes the role of neuropeptides, which are small molecules that act as messengers between the body and the brain, in the communication between emotions and physical health. She makes a compelling case that the body is our unconscious. In fact, numerous experts believe that the mind-body is a false, and potentially misleading dichotomy. It's really one integrated system. We now know that cells have the capacity to signal wirelessly. So, while the brain seems to be the center of cognition it is massively influenced by potentially every cell in the body."

Shane and his team were taking all this in and realizing its importance.

Sherlock picked up the conversation. "My friend Dr. Rankin has even taken this a step further, and argues that the different parts of ourselves are what he calls 'Programmed Personas.' He suggests that there is a specific multi-cellular programing that underpins our different sides, or moods, or expressions of ourselves, that for the most part are formed by habit. And the implication is that we could, at least theoretically, change any part of ourselves that we did not want. For example, if someone was constantly putting themselves down, like apparently Nat used to do, the cellular programming underpinning that side of Nat, or that persona, could be decoded, and thus changed very significantly."

Mary responded. "That sounds a bit like an alter ego that comes from severe trauma, you know, multiple personality disorder. Although I believe that there are quite a few scientists who don't buy into that at all. It seems a little fanciful to me."

Watson was quick to interject.

"Don't dismiss the idea of alter egos, or even personas as Rankin theorizes in his Programmed Persona Theory. I have seen such cases, and those alter egos have their own physical characteristics. I have seen some women with multiple personality disorder have male alter egos, and some men have female alter egos. I assure you it is very real, and I believe these 'personas' have specific multicellular mind-body programming that underpins their state," said Watson convincingly.

Mary nodded in acknowledgement of Watson's comments while wondering what they might have to do with the case of Nat's demise.

"The approach to data analysis today is a reflection of our symmetry bias. We want to believe there are patterns in life and assume that such patterns exist and can be found by focusing on the past. But that tendency is a function of the human brain. I can assure you that current evidence is much more valuable than past data," said Sherlock. "Current evidence often takes in the nuances of the context whereas generally historical data does not."

"And, of course, there's Bayesian theory which suggests that 'facts' are merely probabilities that are constantly changing as a result of new information and perspectives," Holmes added.

"Yes," said Earl, "Bayes really upset the scientific community with that notion back in the day, didn't he? Challenged the entire rigid notion of determinism."

"Fast forward to today, and quantum mechanics is doing the same thing," said Watson. "We know that some of our cells sometimes follow quantum rather than Newtonian physics. Which means that some things that happen in the body are not easily explainable. There's even strong evidence that cells can signal wirelessly, which in itself is a game changer."

After a brief pause, Sherlock wondered aloud about whether some mysterious quantum process might have been involved in Nat's death. Did the poison create an explosive reaction that resonated throughout his body?

Shane deflected the thought by stating, "In case you're interested, Noel has released his latest projections about the murderer. Rob has informed me that Noel says that there is a more than 90% chance that the murderer is a male."

Holmes expressed interest in the robot's initial proclamation but once again warned about the implicit cognitive bias in making projections before much more data has been accumulated.

"Also, we have to be very sure that just because 90% of murders in the UK are perpetrated by males, that does not mean that THIS one was," said Holmes. "This is a problem with prediction based on regression analysis. Data from the past may be relevant in general to the next 10, 20, or 100 murders, but doesn't necessarily say anything about any one particular case. After all, 10% of murders in the UK are committed by females," said Holmes. "Perhaps this was one of them."

"I appreciate your perception, Mr. Holmes. It is certainly true that we scientists can be biased towards the big picture," said Mary.

"What about Ron's disappearance? Surely that makes him the prime suspect?" said Earl, changing the subject and drawing a chorus of agreement from the others.

There was a long pause. Sherlock looked at Watson and then spoke again.

"Ron is no longer a suspect in this matter. We have spoken to MI6 and they confirmed with us that Ron was on a call with them from just before midnight until after three in the morning, the timeframe during which Nat died. It is also apparent that there has been a possible security breach that has affected all potential communications. In an abundance of caution, we decided that the important documents we need to inspect had to be collected manually. We asked Ron to go get them. He should be back shortly."

"What sort of communication breach?" asked Shane. "Why didn't you tell me this before?" he snapped angrily.

Watson asked the assembled team to get out their phones and he examine them for their history of recent calls.

"We are concerned that someone or some agency may have interfered with your phones and manipulated some of the data, like call records, specifically from around the time of Nat's death." "Obviously, we have checked Nat's phone and found no record of any calls just prior to his death, but we are concerned that such information has been hacked. Such a deletion of records would suggest that someone – probably someone here -- called him just prior to his death, or he called them."

Watson asked for the team to turn on their phones and hand them over for inspection of their call history. Everyone complied readily except Earl.

"This feels like an invasion of my privacy," he said, handing over his phone.

Watson checked each phone's call history. There was no record of any calls on any of the devices within two hours of Nat's passing.

"How do you know this hack wasn't just a technical failure rather than a pre-meditated act?" asked Mary.

"That's possible, but we have to currently regard this as suspicious until some other cause has been verified," responded Holmes, silently noting Mary's objection.

"How do we even know that the devices have been disrupted? I don't think you have any worthwhile evidence," proclaimed Earl.

"How do we even know that Nat was poisoned?" he objected.

"We are still not entirely certain that is the case. We can only say at this point that poison was detected," said Holmes.

"What are the other possibilities?" asked Mary.

"At this point, we can only speculate," said Holmes. "Anyway, when Ron returns with the information that we need we will sit with each of you individually and ask you more questions."

"Has Noel reached any conclusions?" asked Rue.

"Yes. Noel thinks it is unlikely that Nat was poisoned, as fewer than one percent of murders occur that way," said Rob, at which point Sherlock intervened to prevent potentially more sensitive information being released to the perpetrator, whom he believed was sitting right in front of him in this very room.

"Our update is complete, you are now dismissed," Holmes said.

Everyone left except Rob, to share Noel's current perspective in more detail. Once the room was cleared, Rob opened up about Noel's insights.

"Noel is skeptical that Nat was poisoned because fewer than 1% of homicides are conducted that way. However, he did note that if Nat was poisoned the chances of the murderer being a woman increase almost four-fold. While only 10% of murders are executed by women, 40% of murders by poison are conducted by women."

"Noel also surmises that while money is a common cause of murder, that doesn't apply here, and the motive is more likely to be a matter of revenge or jealousy."

At his point there was a knock on the door and Sandra entered with a tray full of food and some tea.

"I'm sure you blokes are hungry. God, it's past nine o'clock. I made you some tea and some sandwiches. There are also some biscuits. I hope this will be okay," said Sandra putting down the overloaded tray.

The men thanked her for her thoughtfulness and sat down for some well-earned refreshment.

Chapter Twelve

Tuesday 9:30pm

"In everything one thing is impossible: rationality."
Friedrich Nietzsche

As the detectives finished dinner, Watson received a text message from Ron.

"Where is he?" Holmes asked.

"He says he's about fifteen minutes away and will deliver the files as soon as he arrives," Watson said.

"Perfect. Why don't we go ahead and talk with Mary while we wait?"

"I'll have Shane call her and tell her to come to the den," Watson said.

Mary was a very determined and beautiful woman. She stood out in any crowd because of both characteristics. Holmes observed her carefully as she entered the room.

"Please take a seat Dr. Heald," said Watson. "We just want to learn a bit more about you and how you came to be where you are today."

"I understand," said Mary.

"Okay," said Watson, taking a deep breath. "Please tell us a little about your family."

"My father was a businessman. He was into banking technology. My mother was a biology teacher who loved playing the piano. I was an only child, and as a child I loved acting and ballet. For most of my childhood years we lived not too far from here, up the road in Northampton."

"How did you do in school?" asked Watson.

"I could be very intense. I questioned everything. A definite skeptic. But as I said, I enjoyed ballet and especially acting. I was in several school plays."

"Was there much of a spiritual element in your family life?"

"Both my parents were Jewish, but they weren't into it much. Eventually my mother converted to Catholicism. She took me to church, but I was really only interested in the boys at that time. You know, 'Ah, men!'"

"Do you believe in heaven?" asked Holmes.

"Well, that's a very strange question, if I may say so," said Dr. Heald. "Why do you ask?"

"I have my reasons, and I will explain them in due course. But for now, could you answer the question?" said Holmes.

"Honestly, I'm not sure how to answer. However, if you insist on a definitive answer, I will say that I don't believe in heaven."

"Did you have a lot of boyfriends?" asked Holmes, changing the topic and looking directly into Mary's stunning brown eyes.

"Yes, a few, but I was very focused on my studies, too. Early on in school I found the homework pretty easy, but as I progressed into college, I was very determined to do well and spent a lot of my time studying."

"How did you get interested in bioengineering?" asked Watson.

"It was partly through my mother's interest in biology, but also some classes that I took in college. It just fascinated me."

"Did you ever consider pursuing a career in ballet, acting, or even modelling?" asked Holmes.

"I'm reminded of a line that has always resonated with me. I can't recall who said it, I think it was a famous actress."

"What's the quote?" asked Holmes.

"Any girl can be glamorous; all you have to do is stand still and look stupid," said Mary.

Watson chuckled.

Mary then explained how she continued with her studies and got advanced degrees at the University of London.

"I got distracted while writing my doctoral thesis," she volunteered. "I met a guy named Frank and was intrigued with him. He wanted to marry me, but I just didn't feel that committed. It was the closest I ever got to falling in love."

The revelation was a conundrum for the investigators both of whom had assumed that this lovely, brilliant woman would have had many suitors.

Mary explained that she had not even had a serious relationship with a man in the twenty years since her relationship with Frank.

"I have a lot of friends and a decent social life – as social as I want."

"What do you make of Nat's death?"

"It's unfathomable to me. I am very sad about his death." There was a pause before Mary spoke again.

"You do know that Nat was gay, don't you?"

The investigators looked startled.

"What evidence do you have for that?" asked Holmes.

"We stayed up late one night and started talking about our personal lives. Honestly, looking back now, I think we might have had a bit too much to drink. Anyway, he told me he was gay but didn't want anyone else to know. But, of course, I think everyone else did know, although I personally never mentioned this to anyone."

"How did they know?" asked Watson.

"You can't be in a community of smart people for years and expect them not to draw conclusions about you," said Mary. "It's a hypothesis because I certainly haven't spoken to them about it, just an educated hunch."

"Do you think that any of the team, or anyone else involved in the project, somehow held his homosexuality against Nat?" asked Holmes.

"I seriously doubt that. But I can't say for sure," said Mary. "I'm yet to be convinced that he didn't commit suicide. That seems more likely to me than him being murdered. He was always hard on himself, you know."

"When was the last time you saw him?" asked Holmes.

"Last night before we all retired for the evening, about twenty-four hours ago. Wow, it seems much longer than that now. We had just finished a meeting about the successful operation against the Chinese. We all said goodnight to each other and went to our respective rooms."

"How did he seem before he retired?" asked Sherlock.

"He seemed okay. It's always difficult to judge how Nat is feeling." The she paused and corrected herself. "It was always difficult to judge how Nat *was* feeling," solemnly emphasizing the past tense.

"Your room is directly opposite from Nat's. Did you hear or see anything suspicious last evening, or even any other evening?" Holmes continued.

"I have been trying to remember if I did. But honestly, if you have to force yourself to remember something, chances are that your memory is going to be unreliable. I have racked my brains but I'm not coming up with anything."

"I am going to ask you something, Dr. Heald, and please, I need you to keep this a secret from anyone else. Do you understand?" said Holmes earnestly.

"Yes, of course," said Mary.

"Do you know why Nat would have money stashed under his mattress?" asked Holmes.

"Now that is a question I can verifiably answer," said Mary.

"And the answer is…?" Asked Holmes.

At that point there was a knock at the door. It was Sandra telling them that Ron had arrived and wanted to see them immediately.

The interruption signaled the end of the meeting, for now.

"We'll catch up with you tomorrow, Dr. Heald. Thanks so much for your comments," said Sherlock.

Mary passed Ron in the doorway, giving him wide berth and not making eye contact.

"What's up with her?" Ron asked as he entered the room.

"In the eyes of your other team members, you're suspect number one because you left the scene of the crime," Watson said.

"Well, I had no choice, I was following M16 orders."

"We know. It doesn't matter what the others think," Holmes said.

"I have told them that you are no longer a person of interest in the investigation. Yes, Shane was annoyed that you left without telling him, but hopefully he'll understand," said Holmes.

"What did you find out?" asked Holmes.

"The official orders are to carry on business as usual during the investigation. Any requests to leave the campus must be forwarded to MI6. By the way MI6 will be here tomorrow," said Ron.

"Jim Faulkner is the leader of the team. He is a great guy. Have you worked with him before?" asked Ron.

Holmes replied that most of the collaboration they had done with government agencies had been with MI5, the body responsible for domestic security. MI6 was involved with foreign intelligence.

"Well, you'll find it interesting, I'm sure," Ron said. "And Colleen the psych expert is also very competent."

"Let's review the key details about Nat's life," said Ron as he pulled out a large folder.

Ron recounted the details of the folder.

"Nat's dad was a civil servant, and his mother Ethel was from an Irish family. Nat grew up in Maida Vale in London and then later in Guildford, Surrey. His first school headmistress apparently noted his extraordinary genius even at that age."

"He enjoyed long distance running and cycling. He had an older brother, Bill, and was considered very smart. He went to two boarding schools before moving on to King's College, Cambridge. He performed exceptionally in college and was a believer in the spirit residing in the body. He also liked to consult fortune tellers, one of whom told him at a young age that he would be recognized as a scientific genius."

"We know that he could have a good sense of humor, but he also had a dark side that often emerged when he was struggling with solving a problem. I guess he was so used to getting things right and easily reaching conclusions that not being able to do that frustrated him," added Ron.

"Is there any evidence that he had ever been suicidal?" Watson asked.

"That's a difficult question to answer. If he ever was, I don't think he let anyone know about it. There's no evidence of him ever making an attempt on his life," said Ron. "Anyway, haven't we dismissed the idea that he committed suicide?"

"Nothing is dismissed until it is no longer possible," interrupted Sherlock.

"We'll have more information, hopefully by tomorrow, or at least once an official autopsy is completed," said Watson.
The rest of the file was reviewed and revealed nothing that wasn't known already about Nat.

"Does it say anywhere whether Nat believed there was a heaven?" asked Sherlock?

Again, this question prompted looks of confusion, especially by Watson. Seeing this, Sherlock raised his brow indicating to his colleague not to challenge the question or its purpose.

Ron replied that there didn't seem to be anything in the files about that, but his personal belief was that Nat did indeed believe in heaven.

"Is there anything else in all those files that we should be immediately aware of?" asked Holmes.

"Maybe a couple of things, though how relevant they are, I'm not sure," said Ron.

"The first is that we might pay more attention to the night receptionist, Sandra. On further examination we have found that there are some questionable things in her history. She was a receptionist at a hotel in Lincolnshire where there was a big international meth lab operating on the fourth floor. There was a large police operation involved in that case, but she was never implicated in the operation. However, the details suggest that it would have been unlikely that she didn't know what was going on."

Sherlock thanked Ron and agreed that they would talk to Sandra in more depth. However, Ron himself admitted some doubt that she was involved. He couldn't imagine what possible motive Sandra would have.

Holmes said he was reminded of a quote, but he couldn't remember the origin and who stated it.

"It's relevant to this case and Sandra's possible involvement. It goes something like this. 'Sometimes it is the people no one imagines anything of who do the things that no one can imagine. ...'"

Ron and Watson both nodded in agreement.

Holmes then asked Ron who had recommended or hired Sandra. Ron said that he certainly didn't have a say in her being employed at the Range, and thought that was delegated to a different department at the Defense Department. However, Ron had checked and found that, at least from the records, Sandra had passed all the required background checks and had the requisite clearances.

"Oh, and I did find out something surprising about Earl, but I have no idea if it has any relevance," said Ron changing the subject.

"What should we know about Earl?" asked Watson.

"Apparently, he is quite the ladies' man. He has had numerous relationships since his wife died a few years ago."

"Do you think that he and Mary have had anything going on between them?" asked Watson.

"It's possible, but I have no evidence that's the case. I guess only time will tell," suggested Ron.

Ron mentioned one final detail that he thought was inconsequential. He said that all of them had received confirmation of their hiring by letter and these were meant to be in the files, but he couldn't find them.

"So, all of the persons of interest are missing a letter," repeated Holmes.

Ron assented and with that the three of them retired for the evening.

Chapter Thirteen

Wednesday: 7:30am

"It is the consistency of the information that matters for a good story, not its completeness. Indeed, you will often find that knowing little makes it easier to fit everything you know into a coherent pattern."
Daniel Kahneman

The investigators were up at the crack of dawn, eating breakfast in the dining room and summarizing their findings so far. It was going to be a busy morning interviewing the other members of the team and catching up with Noel's prognostications.

Before they got started, Watson and Holmes scanned the news over their tea. Of course, the international conflict was front page news, but it was another piece that stirred Sherlock's ire.

"Bloody hell! Listen to this, Watson!" exclaimed Holmes as he prepared to read a headlined story.

"'AI offers promising cancer cure!' What the hell! Everything is now presented as an AI development. Who programmed the damned AI? Humans, of course. And of course, these articles are never framed as a combination of human and artificial intelligence. And it was humans who not only programmed these robots but also did the research so that contemporary machines could help! Good God!!"

Before Watson could interrupt Sherlock's tirade, Holmes spoke again.

"Don't people realize that it is humans that are programming these things! Yes, imperfect, biased humans, with their own agenda, not perfectly logical, independent minds, operating for the good of humanity!! How can people be so stupid!"

Sherlock wasn't finished.

"And look at this one. 'AI finds missing plane.' For God's sake it used a damned human-designed tracking system that was programmed by humans. Humans would have, and did, find the missing plane. This obsession with AI is getting absurd!"

"Sherlock, please watch your blood pressure," said Watson.

"No worries there, Watson, I have AI on my wrist protecting my health! I'm sure AI is keeping me alive! I mean AI is responsible for everything, even my breathing! Can you imagine what this would have been like as the industrial revolution developed technology?"

"'New technology creates the Adventures of Huckleberry Finn for Mark Twain!' Oh my God, he used a *typewriter*, which was clearly instrumental in the author's creation. A typewriter creates an amazing fictional character!"

"You seem to be very angry and irritated by all the attention artificial intelligence is getting," said Watson. "AI for an eye, Bluetooth for a tooth?" he opined.

"Okay, doctor. Let me take a few minutes to breathe and calm down and we can get going," Holmes responded.

Earl, Ron, and Mary, sitting at a nearby table, couldn't help but over hear Sherlock's tirade. As Holmes tried to relax Earl reopened the discussion.

"You seem pretty mad at technology in general and AI in particular," commented Earl. "Are you conscious of all the possibilities AI brings to the world?"

Holmes responded. "Consciousness. Here we are talking about the possibility of artificial consciousness, and we don't even understand our own consciousness. We don't know the full extent of the mind-body."

"Have you heard about Daniel Kish?" asked Watson to Earl as well as Mary and Ron.

Mary knew but Earl and Ron did not, prompting him to continue.

"Daniel became blind before he was two. He actually had his eyes removed at the age of thirteen months because of cancer. For some reason he started making clicking sounds with his tongue. And before long he had learned the skill of echolocation, an amazing skill usually attributed to dolphins and bats. Daniel could translate the echoes created by the environment to his clicking into visual representation of the world around him, allowing him to do things like ride a bike, even though he was blind. When researchers studied his brain, they found that the visual areas of his brain that were normally dormant in people with no eyes had connected to the auditory areas of his brain, to create this amazing skill. He has now taught this skill to more than five hundred people."

Earl and Ron were amazed at the idea of human echolocation. And then Watson posed another question.

"How many digits can people remember?" asked Watson.

"I know the answer to that one," said Mary. "It's between 5 and 9, the number seven plus or minus two, as established by the psychologist George Miller in the 1950s."

Watson acknowledged that was correct for the average person but then asked whether anyone knew what the record was for digit recall.

"20?" suggested Ron.

"No, it's more like 1000," said Earl.

There was a sarcastic mumble at Earl's absurd suggestion. How could anyone remember a thousand numbers in the right order?

"The answer is," said Watson slowly, "….100,000."

After the gasps of amazement slowly faded, Watson provided more information.

"A Japanese gentleman Akira Haraguchi, achieved that feat, which took him 16 hours, in 2006."

"Wait a minute," interjected Mary. "Haraguchi was using a system to calculate the numbers rather than remembering them. It was ana amazing feat but I'm not sure it was memorization,"

Watson responded. "Okay, how about this one. Have you heard of Timur Gareyev? He's a Grand Master Chess Champion. In 2016, he played 48 games of chess simultaneously while blindfolded. It took him nineteen hours and he did it while riding an exercise bike. He won 35, drew 7 and lost 6."

"I don't think we humans really appreciate what we are capable of. The mind-body is an incredible computer. It's ability to change and adapt, neuroplasticity, is incredible and we probably haven't even scratched the surface yet. In combination with technology, it is almost unfathomable to imagine what we will be able to do in the years, decades, and centuries ahead," concluded Dr. Watson.

"However, the key phrase there is *in combination with technology*," said Holmes. "We need to focus on human capabilities, and motives, as much, if not more, than we do on the development of artificial intelligence."

Just then, Shane entered the room.

"It's time to get started with the interviews of the morning," he said.

Earl was the first on the list. Watson and Holmes told him they would meet with him in the office appointed by Shane in five minutes.

"I'll be there shortly," said Earl.

Earl was described by those who knew him as outwardly charming and gentle, but that outward appearance seemed to conceal a highly energized temperament. Everyone who met him would agree that he had an amazingly high level of intellectual energy. Some people even called him child-like and obstinate.

Earl told the investigators that he had grown up in the London suburb of Harrow. His father and uncle were in the electrical business and his mother loved music.

"My mom could be very demanding," said Earl. "She insisted I learn to play the piano before I even got into school. As much as I dreaded it, I did enjoy it. In fact, music is one of my passions."

Watson commented how Mary had also been passionate about music growing up, too, through her mother's obsession with it.

"Music is non-linguistic and takes us to a totally different landscape of unexplained passion and perception. That's why it can be the basis of both creativity and intelligence," said Earl.

"What about your family?"

"I have a sister Maria," Earl replied.

Earl told the investigators that he didn't like his early school years.

"I intuitively rejected rote learning. It was boring and useless. I was imaginative, and couldn't stand sitting in class for hours, literally bored out of my mind. I got into a lot of trouble as a result, but fortunately, or otherwise, my parents agreed with me. Play and imagination is far more important than knowledge."

Earl then went on to explain that as he got older, he found subjects that engaged his intelligence and his imagination. And although he enjoyed and excelled at physics, he always thought his future lay in music or philosophy. But by the time he went to university, science was his passion. And soon there was another passion.

"I met Susan in college, and we instantly hit it off. In fact, my sister was dating her brother at the time. I loved studying with Susan. We were married for several years before we parted ways. She was frustrated with my cheating on her."

This stimulated questions about Earl's spiritual background. He told Watson and Holmes that he was born into a Catholic family.

Watson silently rolled his eyes as he anticipated Holmes next question.

"Earl, do you believe in heaven?" asked Sherlock.

"Yes, actually I do," said Earl. "I know that might sound irrational to some, but I do embrace the concept."

Holmes mentioned that he knew Earl and Susan had divorced and encouraged Earl to talk about his adult life.

"After I divorced Susan, I married Ella. And as you may know, Ella died several years ago from heart problems."

"Have you ever considered remarrying?" asked Watson.

"No, I don't have time for any of that. I'm too obsessed with my work. Don't have much of a social life, but that's fine with me," said Earl.

"What was your relationship with Nat like?" asked Holmes.

"I'd say we got on pretty well. There were some things that we didn't agree on, but for the most part our relationship was cordial."

"What didn't you agree on?" asked Holmes.

"Technical stuff. He was enamored by quantum theory, and I am not. So, he mused about non-locality and superposition and all that kind of spooky stuff. If that's true, then he is probably alive in some other universe as we speak. If we could only find that version of him, he could tell us what happened to him last night," Earl added sarcastically.

"Do you think he was killed, or do you feel there's some other explanation?" asked Watson.

"Well, I can tell you for sure, I didn't kill him. Personally, I think it was an accident or possibly a suicide. I simply cannot imagine any members of our team wanting to take him out."

There was a pause before Earl added, "However, now I think about it, have you questioned Sandra, the night receptionist?"

"What makes you say that?" asked Holmes.

"I have a funny feeling about her. I can't really put my finger on it exactly – just a funny feeling. I suspect she could be quite confrontational and even a little mean."

Holmes and Watson shared a glance as Earl's idea was aired.

"Well, killing someone is being more than a little mean, don't you think?" asked Sherlock. "And what possible motive could she have?"

Earl shrugged off the question. There was another pause after which Earl spoke again.

"I'm not sure about Sandra. Something is not quite right there," he offered.

There was no response to Earl's thoughts about the receptionist at which point, Earl stood up.

"Are we finished then?" Earl suggested.

"Yes, that's all for now. If we need to follow-up, we'll let you know," said Watson. "MI6 will want to do a more extensive interview, but that's all for now."

"Why do you think he is so suspicious of Sandra?" Watson asked after Earl had left.

"Not sure. Perhaps she rejected his advances?" suggested Holmes.

"Could be," agreed Watson.

Chapter Fourteen

Wednesday 9:00am

"In believing too much in rationality, our contemporaries have lost something."
Krzysztof Kieslowski

As Earl left, he passed Rue in the hallway heading to Holmes' office.

"Hello beautiful," said Earl as he saw Rue. "I'm sure you will dazzle them with your charm."

Rue rolled her eyes, walked on and then greeted the investigators.

The detectives already knew that Rue Carime grew up in Wembley, North London. She had an older sister called Sophia. Her father was a mathematics and physics teacher at Harrow County school for boys. Her mother Barbara operated a local kindergarten but retired when Rue was born.

"Can you give us some more details on your early life?" asked Watson.

Rue reflected for a moment.

"My dad had made some risky investments that had failed, so to supplement their income they rented out a couple of rooms to boarders at my dad's school. They were boys, of course. It made the house pretty crowded and occasionally noisy and stressful. Fortunately, that only happened for a couple of years when I was very young. I don't think it would have been quite so easy as I matured into a teenager."

"That must have been tough for you as the youngest," commented Holmes.

"To some extent, but it gets worse. My sister Sophia died when I was eleven. And three years later my mother Barbara died of cancer."

"What effect did that have on you?" asked Sherlock.

"Well, I gave up my belief in God and became agnostic. My mother was a devout Protestant and was constantly praying for healing during her illness but after she died, I lost my faith."

"Do you believe in heaven?" asked Holmes predictably.

"After both my sister and mother died, I wanted to believe in it. I wanted to know that they were together in a safe, loving place. That we would all be united one day. I love the idea, but do I believe in it now? No, I don't," said Rue.

"What about your father?"

"He died three years ago. He was almost eighty."

"What sort of relationship did you have with him?"

"We were pretty close. Of course, he was devastated, too, by the loss of his teenage daughter and then his wife. He had dementia."

"The record shows that you were very good in school, especially the social sciences," said Watson changing the subject.

"Yes, I loved it, and of course, my dad inspired me, too. And Sophia was very good at it too and it increased our bond and love for each other," Rue smiled elegantly.

The investigators said nothing but encouraged her to continue.

"After the loss of my mother and sister, I was very depressed, and I needed a break before starting my studies at Cambridge. So, I decided to do just that for a couple of years," Rue said earnestly.

"What did you do to earn some money?"

"My dad had some relatives who lived not far away in Pinner. They needed help with Jack, a disabled child, and so I became a nurse's aide and a home school tutor for him. It worked well. For the most part."

There was an uncomfortable pause which signaled an oncoming revelation.

"Jack had a brother my age, Rich. We became very close. Actually, he was my first love. But it didn't work out. At one point I thought we were getting married, but the whole thing collapsed. I left my job and soon after resumed my studies," Rue said quietly. "I was still a teenager, what did I know?"

"That must have been difficult," said Watson.

"I was devastated for a short while and then I put my attention elsewhere. You know hindsight removes you from those romantic dopamine moments and it is easier to disconnect from the emotion, allowing you to justify events as the best outcome." "Then you resumed your studies at Cambridge, right?" checked Watson.

"Yes, I did. I took some part time work with a charity and became very interested in organizational psychology. It just seemed natural for me."

"And it was at Cambridge that you met Peter, correct?" asked Watson.

Rue nodded sadly.

There was another long silence. Both investigators knew about Peter's death some ten years earlier, when he was killed while biking on a very wet highway near Cambridge.

"You know what happened to him, right?" asked Rue.

"I'm so sorry," said Watson.

"Yes, he loved biking in the country but for some reason I could never get into that," said Rue with a solemn smile. "I'm not a country girl."

"Rue, you have had a difficult life. How has all this tragedy affected you?" asked Watson.

"To be honest, for the most part, it's made me stronger. Suffering can teach you a lot. I have adapted. Since Peter died, I have been very reluctant to chase relationships, as you might imagine. But life for the most part is good. I love what I am doing here. I periodically am on medication, but I get by and take pride in my work."

Both Holmes and Watson were impressed with Rue's strength and authenticity.

"What was your relationship with Nat like?" asked Holmes.

"He was a gentleman. I never had any problem with him," said Rue confidently. "We trusted each other implicitly."

"What do you make of this situation?" asked Holmes.

In similar manner to all those who were asked this question, Rue seemed to be perplexed by the whole incident.

"Well, I think several of us wonder whether this was an accident or, perhaps…even suicide," said Rue almost reluctantly. She paused on the mention of the word suicide. Eventually she continued, "It seems inconceivable that he was murdered, well, at least by anyone here. I can't imagine any of the scientists harming Nat. They appreciated his work so much. I'm sure some of the others have told you that Ron can get a bit bent out of shape at times, but I find it hard to believe that he had anything to do with it. Anyway, you have ruled Ron out already, right?"

Holmes nodded in the affirmative and determined it was time to meet with Rob.

"Thank you, Dr. Carime. If you think of anything that could be helpful, please don't hesitate to reach out to us," said Holmes as the meeting ended.

Prior to their next meeting, Watson called Natural Exterminators to find out more about their pesticides. He put his phone on speaker so Holmes could hear the conversation and dialed the number. A young lady answered.

"Nat Exterminators. How can I help you?"

"I'm sorry who do you say this is?" asked Watson, a little thrown by the coincidental conflagration of concepts.

"Natural Exterminators," clarified the lady on the other end of the phone. "How can I help you?"

Watson explained that he would like to speak with an executive or engineer and ask them about the pesticides that the company used and their recent visit to the Range. The lady at the other end of the phone asked Watson to wait while she found the appropriate person and put him on hold.

A man eventually picked up the phone and identified himself as Ryan. Watson explained that he wished to know what pesticides the company used, especially for indoor use. Ryan ran through the list of the chemicals that the company used, which did not include strychnine.

"What about strychnine?" asked Watson.

"No sir, that has been banned in the United Kingdom since 2005. It was used a lot before then but declared too dangerous. We haven't used it since."

"Well, I'm calling about your recent visit to the Range," said Watson.

There was a pause before Ryan responded.

"Can you hold on a second, sir, I need to check something with my boss," said Ryan.

Holmes and Watson shared intrigued glances.

Watson waited patiently and before too long another man was on the 'phone. He introduced himself as Aram, the owner of Natural Exterminators.

"What's your connection with the Range?" Aram asked.

"My name is John Watson and I'm a private contractor doing some work there. I had some questions about the moles that seemed to be running wild there recently."

"So, you're nothing to do with the government, then?" asked the owner.

"Good lord, no," said Watson. "Why do you ask?"

"Actually, are you Dr. John Watson?" asked Aram.

"Yes, I am."

"Well, you probably don't remember me, but I used to live near Baker Street. You might remember seeing me walk a big black dog," said Aram.

"Oh, yes. You're that big, handsome muscular guy," recalled Watson, trying to use this convenient truth to help him get the answers he was looking for.

"Well, I'll tell you this but please don't share it with anyone," said Aram.

"No, of course not."

Both Holmes and Watson were intrigued to find out what was about to be revealed.

"Okay then," Aram said hesitantly.

"A few weeks ago, the lady that runs the place called us and said she was having a big problem with the rodents. She asked us specifically whether we could spray some strychnine to get control of the problem. Well, I told her that we couldn't do that. She then asked whether we could supply her with some strychnine, and she would take care of it. I told her that strychnine was no longer legal to use but she insisted, saying she wouldn't tell anyone else about it. So, we have been giving her some when we do our monthly visits. On our recent visit we gave her the second lot she asked for. She thanked us and said it was beginning to work. We have told her to be very careful with it, especially if there are children and youngsters around. There's been recent research that shows that kids living in an environment where that stuff is used are at risk for serious health hazards. Apparently, it impacts their ability to breathe and all sorts of things. She assured us that there were no kids there at all, and the place was largely empty."

"Well, thank you for that, Aram. It will remain a secret, I assure you. One last thing what is the name of the lady who asked you to do this?" said Watson.

Aram said he couldn't remember but would go check the records and be back in a few seconds. And about a minute later he was back.

"The woman's name is Sandra," said Aram.

"Thank you so much, I really appreciate your time," said Watson before hanging up.

"What the heck is Sandra doing with that strychnine?" wondered Watson out loud.

"Killing those damn rodents, no doubt," said Holmes. "And maybe one of them is called Nat."

Chapter Fifteen

Wednesday: 10:00am

"The comfort zone is the great enemy to creativity;
moving beyond it necessitates intuition, which in turn
configures new perspectives and conquers fears."
Dan Stevens

Rob sat down to be interviewed, clearly nervous. He was biting his nails and had a tense expression.

"I know the events of the past couple of days have everyone on edge," Watson said. "Just relax, as much as you can, and tell us a little about yourself."

Rob talked about his father, a professor of physiology at the University of Sussex, and his mom, who came from a successful business background. As a result, his life growing up was comfortable. He talked about how he and his younger brother George loved playing sports, especially cricket. In fact, George had played professionally and Rob at an amateur level.

Sherlock asked Rob about whether religion or spirituality played a part in his family's life. Rob answered that the family was effectively agnostic and didn't subscribe to any religion.

"At one point I was into Buddhism when I was in college," Rob admitted, "but never really followed it up."

"Do you believe in heaven?" asked Sherlock as Watson tried hard not to change his expression.

"No, not really, not anymore. When I was into Buddhism, I did believe in reincarnation, but I don't anymore," answered Rob.

When invited to reveal more about his personal life, Rob continued.

"I met Margaret, who was the sister of a colleague of mine, while in my first job as an assistant professor. We had three children. They all have careers in science and technology and two of them live in the United States."

"And your wife?" asked Sherlock

"She left me five years ago. The more I got involved in robotics, the more distanced we became."

Watson asked about Dr. Rob's overall health.

"I was diagnosed with an episode of depression a few years ago and put on some anti-depressants. I'm still on them until this day. You know those things are damned hard to come off."

When asked about his relationship with Nat, Rob claimed that it was very good.

"Our fascination with robots and artificial intelligence drew us together. We were constantly sharing ideas about new developments in tech and where artificial intelligence was going."

"Did you have compatible ideas about AI development?" asked Holmes.

"Nat was a bit more conservative on that issue. He believed there was a limit on what robots could do and that there needed to be a melding of artificial and human intelligence. I believe that robots could surpass human intelligence one day. I know that sounds scary, but I think the chance of robots taking over is a serious possibility."

Sherlock responded. "Well, if AI continues to require training and fundamental direction and purpose from humans, surely that means that ultimately it is humans we need to be wary of, not their mechanical sidekicks? Aren't we witnessing that already? Technology gives humanity many options, but of course, some of those options enable the worst sides of human nature. My personal view is that the greatest threat to humanity is humans themselves."

Rob didn't feel the need to respond and simply waited for the next question.

When asked about his views on Nat's relationship with the other team members, Rob surmised that they were generally good and that the team had a good chemistry. Like the others, he acknowledged that Ron could be "a bit frustrating at times," but he didn't think that Ron, or anyone else on the team, had murdered Nat. Like the others, he was more prone to see it as an accident.

"Do you think it could have been suicide?" Holmes asked.

"Not very likely, but more feasible than murder in my view," said Rob, sniffling. "He took everything so damned hard. I could definitely relate to his depression," said Rob moving from sniffles to tears.

"I apologize for getting snarky with you, Mr. Holmes, when we first met. It upsets me when obviously smart people like yourself are dismissive about technology and robotic capabilities. I hope you will allow Noel to aid you in your investigation. It can access a massive amount of data, and while I agree with you, a lot of it will be irrelevant, there could be a gem that could make the difference in resolving this dastardly matter."

"There's no need to apologize Dr. Shine," said Holmes. "I, too, can lose my perspective at times. Critical thinking requires being openminded, if a little cynical. You have to strike the right balance, and that's not always easy to do. So, yes, I'm happy to share information that you can feed to Noel. Let's see what he…it…comes up with."

Rob smiled and offered his outstretched hand to Holmes, who shook it warmly, as Watson looked on with gratitude but a foreboding sense that one, or both sides, were being more than slightly disingenuous.

"There's one thing that you and Noel should know, if you don't already," said Sherlock.

Rob looked at him inquisitively.

"How much do you know about Nat's personal life?" Sherlock asked.

"Well, I know he was an excellent long-distance runner, didn't believe in God, but was quite spiritual," said Rob. "I know he never married but he did tell me he proposed to a young lady earlier in his life, but that didn't work out for him. I know some members of the team think he was gay, but we never discussed that side of life. It wouldn't surprise me if he were indeed gay, but it wouldn't change my view of him as a brilliant and likeable man. He isolated himself a bit more than the rest of us."

There was an awkward silence.

"What are you thinking?" asked Rob.

Before Holmes and Watson spoke further, Rob got the gist of their thoughts, or believed he did.

"Oh, you think Nat was gay. Now, if you're wondering whether he ever implied or suggested some sexual activity with me -- absolutely NOT!"

"I know that is an uncomfortable thought, but often murders involving gay men do spring from misunderstandings about sexual intentions," said Holmes.

"I understand," said Rob. "And it's certainly something that needs to be relayed to Noel. Do you have confirmation that Nat was gay?"

"It's a very distinct possibility, but we would appreciate it if you didn't share this idea with anyone else," said Sherlock.

Rob agreed. "After you have finished your interviews please come down to the lab and I will tell you about Noel's latest analysis." "Thank you again," said Watson.

"My pleasure. Please let me know if there's anything else I can help you with," said Rob before exiting.

The investigators nodded their assent. before moving on with their next assignment, interviewing Sandra, something that now had added importance in view of the recent call with Natural Exterminators. Fortunately, Sandra was staying later in the day after her night shift because of the disruption caused by the recent events.

"Okay, let's talk to the receptionist and see what she has to say about strychnine," said Holmes.

"And maybe pillowcases," added Watson as he left the office.

When Watson found Sandra, he saw her talking to a lady.

"Oh, Dr. Watson, this is Allison, the daytime receptionist I told you about," said Sandra. "I believe you wanted to chat with her."

Watson thanked Sandra and asked her to wait for a few minutes before leaving for the day as they wanted to ask some questions. As Sandra assented, Watson escorted Allison back to the office.

Unfortunately, Allison was not very helpful. She said she couldn't identify whose laundry in general and pillowcases in particular, belonged to whom. When asked about possible tears in pillowcases, she could offer no convincing explanation.

"Sometimes the pillowcases get caught up with the other laundry and I suppose could get torn if someone was trying to untangle them by pulling at them. I haven't seen too many tears in any of the laundry during my time working here," Allison offered.

Allison had very few insights to offer on Nat or his relationships with the other team members.

"He wasn't around much, to be honest. I believe he was working hard most of the time, or else scrolling through social media," said Allison. "When he wasn't working, and when I did see him, he seemed to be scrolling through his phone a lot. I don't see the others do that much."

"Who do you think was closest to him?" asked Holmes.

"That's hard to say. I'm not sure I could honestly say he was close to any of them." Allison stopped to ponder the question further.

"Probably Rue and Mary, maybe even Sandra," she finally offered. "Those are the people that he seemed most relaxed around."

"How did he relate to you?" asked Watson.

"He was cordial, but he also could be very distant. I assumed it was the stress of the work he was doing."

The questioning over, Watson escorted Allison out of the office and invited Sandra in take her place and talk to them.

Chapter Sixteen

Wednesday: 11:00am

"If you look for truth, you may find comfort in the end;
if you look for comfort you will not get either comfort or
truth only soft soap and wishful thinking to begin, and in
the end, despair."
C. S. Lewis

"Thank you for your time, Sandra. I know you have been here a long time after your shift and hopefully you can leave immediately we have finished asking you some questions," said Holmes.

"Yes, it's been quite a long shift," said Sandra.

"Have you had any more thoughts on the situation?" asked Holmes.

"Well, I have been asking myself why Ron would leave like that," Sandra said. "I know he has come back now, but it seems mighty suspicious to me," she volunteered.

Holmes assured Sandra that there was a good explanation for Ron's brief absence and then asked the questions that were on his mind.

"How long have you worked as a hotel receptionist?" Sherlock asked.

"It's been about twenty years now," she said. "Ever since my husband died."

"Oh, I'm sorry to hear about that. What happened?" asked Holmes.

"Fred was a wonderful bloke. The love of my life. I was devastated when he got cancer. I took care of him until he passed away. There was nothing I wouldn't do for him."

"That's nice to hear you had such a great relationship. Sometimes an illness like that can really change a marriage," commented Watson.

"No, that wasn't me or Fred. We really loved each other."

"As you say, you have been working in the hotel business for quite some time now. Have there been any incidents like this one?" asked Holmes.

"No, not really," said Sandra scratching the side of her nose. "A few people getting sick and needing an ambulance, that's about it."

"Have the police ever been involved in any of the properties you worked in?" Holmes continued.

Sandra shook her head. "No, nothing like that. It would have made the job more interesting, that's for sure."

"What are the most challenging parts of this job?" asked Holmes.

"Well, it's a night shift which can mess your life up a bit. The people here are good folks. But there's not much fun. All too bloody serious if you ask me."

"Do you know the details of the work that is done here?" asked Holmes.

"I only know it's to do with that bloody war with China, but apart from that I have no idea what they do. I did have to sign something saying I would not speak or talk about anything that I see or hear here. Didn't really need to because, honestly, I don't understand most of what they are saying."

"Anything else that's difficult about working here?" Sherlock reiterated.

"No, not really. Oh yes, there is one bloody annoying thing," volunteered Sandra.

The investigators eagerly waited for the source of Sandra's frustration.

"The damn rats in the kitchen! Drive me bonkers!"

"How do you deal with that?" asked Watson.

"I leave it to the Exterminator blokes to spray their stuff. It's getting a little better, lately."

"Do you use any spray or anything else yourself to manage the problem?" asked Watson.

"Nah. You wouldn't catch me touching that creepy stuff. I just leave it to the professionals," said Sandra.

After a few more pleasantries, Sandra was dismissed and allowed to leave the premises. By the time she had done so, Watson and Holmes were contemplating why Sandra would lie so openly.   Or had she? Perhaps the previous information about her was wrong? Or perhaps she was indeed lying.

The interview with Sandra now complete, the investigators made their way to the lab to find out Noel's latest insights.

Rob welcomed Holmes and Watson into the robotics center to discuss Noel's latest output and insights into Nat's death.

"I have had Noel process a lot of data not just from the United Kingdom but also from around the world about murders and murderers," said Rob.

"What sort of data?" asked Watson.

"We have looked at many variables. Gender, age, marital status, socio-economic class, marital status, types of weapon used, and other variables like the times of murders."

Sherlock resisted airing his thoughts on the process, wishing to appear cordial with Rob and even Noel. But clearly, Holmes was questioning how valuable any historic data was to a particular current event. He recalled the very words he told Watson before leaving his room for the meeting with Rob: "Trends are fashionable, but fashion has little to do with the truth."

He resisted repeating the phrase again and tried hard to focus as Rob explained the numerous data sources that Noel had analyzed.

Noel had even written a document explaining his reasoning that led him to the conclusion that Nat's killer "was certainly a man."

Data from murders in general showed that men were more likely to be killed by other men. This was even more dramatically shown in the data on gay men who were killed. Hardly any of the hundreds of cases examined of murders of gay men showed that a woman was the murderer.

"I understand the connection, however, surely, we have to be careful in generalizing these data. They are, after all, either hate crimes directed against homosexuals or more typically the result of a sexual liaison gone wrong," said Watson. "I don't think that either of those contexts are relevant here."

"But Dr. Watson, we really don't know that do we? At this point we have no idea about motive, so we can't just assume that this has nothing to do with Nat being gay, or even some misinterpreted sexual gesture," said Rob. "And even if it has nothing to do with Nat's gender orientation, there is still a mass of evidence that suggests a man was the murderer."

"Well, you have certainly compiled a lot of analyses, which is impressive, but I'm not sure it tells us anything particular. Well, not at the moment," said Holmes.

"What do you think, Sherlock? Is the murderer a man or a woman?" asked Rob.

"Well, I'm not sure at this point, but something tells me it was a woman. I'm not certain where that notion is coming from, to be honest, but that's where my intuition is leading me at the moment. However, as we find out more, that notion might change completely. It's just a hypothesis right now, not a fact."

"Is that based on the specific women who are potential suspects, or just some murky feeling?" asked Rob.

"Well, at this moment we have three male persons of interest, Shane, Earl, and yourself, and three female persons of interest, Mary, Rue, and Sandra. I have a very unclear feeling about one of the women," said Holmes.

"Can you identify which woman you think it is?" asked Rob.

"No, not at this precise moment."

"Well, the historical data is against you," said Rob.

"If history repeated itself in exactly the same way in every context, I suspect you would be right. But the only reason people believe that happens is the symmetry bias – we are constantly searching for patterns and are determined to find them even where none exist," said Holmes.

"99% of gay men are killed by men," said Rob, "you can't argue against that, can you?"

"Well, someone with an open mind would either point out that therefore some of the time women are the murderers, and that might indeed be the case in this matter. You're still dealing with probabilities, moreover, ever changing probabilities," said Holmes. "And your argument would suggest that I immediately stop considering any of the women as the suspect and put all my focus on the men."

"Well, I can assure you I had nothing to do with it. And are you certain that Ron has a waterproof alibi?" said Rob.

"Your insistence on the validity of historical data suggests otherwise. You're a man and therefore far more likely than any woman to have committed this ghastly crime. And yes, Ron is no longer a suspect," said Holmes.

"How many of the unsolved murders of gay men might have been committed by women, which is the reason why they are unsolved?" Holmes continued,

"Well, I can't answer that question precisely. I know that in New South Wales in Australia, they were recently tracing about 30 unresolved gay deaths going back more than thirty years. But still, many of those seemed to be hate crimes," said Rob.

"Rob, don't you think that a notion can be a self-fulfilling prophecy? If the police in an area subscribe to the view that gay murders are only committed by men, that is who they will investigate potentially, ignoring female suspects," said Holmes.

"I concede that's a possibility, Sherlock, but even so I still believe that the data strongly suggests a male killer."

Rob continued. "Also, the data that we have found strongly suggests that murders committed after midnight and in the early hours of the morning are committed by males. Again, another almost exclusive phenomenon."
"In addition, murders of men over 50, Nat's age, which constitute about 12 percent of murders both here and worldwide, are almost exclusively male, too. The data is very clear and strong on this point, from whichever perspective. The killer was a male."

At this point Watson interceded to stop the conversation from escalating into something much less helpful.

"A detailed autopsy will be completed within the next twenty-four hours, and that should provide a little more direction. At that point we should have more definite data on whether this was truly a murder or suicide."

"Or even an accident," added Holmes.

"While we are here, Dr. Rob, can you tell me the ways in which you think Noel and AI can help with this investigation?" asked Holmes.

Rob expressed his appreciation at Holmes' question.

"Actually, here is what Noel himself responded when asked this question," said Rob.

Rob handed Holmes some papers.

"AI can play a significant role in solving crimes by assisting law enforcement agencies and investigators in several ways. Here are a few ways in which AI can be helpful in crime-solving:

Predictive Analytics: AI algorithms can analyze vast amounts of data, including historical crime records, demographics, and other relevant information, to identify patterns and predict potential criminal activities or hotspots. This helps law enforcement agencies allocate their resources effectively and proactively prevent crimes.

Facial Recognition: AI-powered facial recognition systems can match surveillance camera footage or images of suspects with existing criminal databases, aiding in the identification and tracking of individuals involved in criminal activities. This technology can be particularly useful in cases where there are limited or no other identifying information available.

Forensic Analysis: AI algorithms can assist forensic experts in analyzing and processing large volumes of digital evidence, such as fingerprints, DNA samples, or video footage. These algorithms can automate the identification and comparison of evidence, speeding up the investigation process and potentially identifying crucial leads or connections.

Natural Language Processing (NLP): NLP techniques enable AI systems to analyze and understand written or spoken language. This can be useful in analyzing witness statements, police reports, or other textual data to extract relevant information, identify potential suspects, or uncover hidden connections between different cases.

Data Mining and Link Analysis: AI can efficiently mine and analyze vast amounts of data from various sources, including social media, financial transactions, phone records, and public databases. By applying link analysis techniques, AI can identify relationships between individuals, uncover hidden connections, and generate leads that might otherwise be challenging to discover manually.

Pattern Recognition: AI algorithms can identify and analyze patterns in crime data, such as modus operandi or similarities between cases, helping investigators link seemingly unrelated crimes and identify potential serial offenders.

Risk Assessment and Early Intervention: AI systems can help assess the risk of reoffending by analyzing individual and contextual factors. This information can aid in determining appropriate sentencing, probation, or intervention strategies to prevent future crimes.

It is important to note that while AI can be a powerful tool in crime solving, its effectiveness depends on the quality and quantity of data available, as well as the ethical considerations and legal frameworks surrounding its use. Human expertise and judgment remain essential in the investigative process, and AI should be viewed as a supportive tool rather than a substitute for human decision-making."

Sherlock and Watson read the computer-generated statement.

Watson was the first to speak.

"Well, as far as forensic analytics and data processing are concerned, why is AI better than human intelligence? Human experts in this field know what data to consider and how it may relate to the crime. I certainly can understand if one was looking at a multi-crime scene with numerous incidents in numerous locations, complex data analysis might be useful, but I'm not convinced it is any better than an expert's review and analysis."

Rob had no time to respond before Holmes weighed in.

"Moreover, when analyzing data, a human expert is doing more than just trying to collect the dots before even connecting them."

Rob looked perplexed and invited Holmes to continue, although he didn't need inviting.

"For example, suppose you want to collect data on your weight because you're concerned you're getting too heavy. You get on the scale and are given the data; 14 stone, or 196 pounds. However, if that is less than you thought you weighed, a rush of satisfaction will likely have you reflecting on what you have been doing right that has resulted in that loss of pounds. Conversely, if you weigh more than you hoped, you will likely feel some disappointment and review what you have been doing and what could be improved. In other words, humans typically don't just record data, they think about it: the context and the implications, and they often do so with emotions that helps weight the significance of the data. I don't think computers do that."

"Well, some AI could do that if it were so programmed, but I hear what you're saying," Rob responded.

"Similarly, natural language processing can be done very effectively by human experts. Indeed, it is the human experts that write the programs that train the robots. AI can simulate that human processing, but I don't think it adds anything special to it. And I would say the same about data mining, although I do agree that some AI could do it faster than human experts, and that could be significant in some cases," added Holmes.

"Honestly, I believe the same comments apply to data mining and link analysis. It's great that AI can simulate human expertise, but I don't think that means it can surpass it," added Watson.

"So, you can see, Dr. Rob, why I am not sure Noel can add anything that a human expert can't. There's value in that it might match human expertise, of course, but we need to keep the right perspective," added Holmes. "Two things that are most overrated by humans: logic and speed."

The investigation had temporarily reached an impasse. Holmes and Noel had different ideas of who the perpetrator was, and the reasons for their actions. Noel believed that the perpetrator was almost certain to be a male, motivated by some type of vengeance. Sherlock believed that the perpetrator was more likely to be a woman, motivated by more personal reasons. Still, Holmes being Holmes, he was still not convinced about anything in the case, including his current perceptions.

As Watson, Holmes, and Dr. Rob mused about the contradictions, Khang popped into Sherlock's mind. This spurred another thought.

"Watson, you recently talked about that predictive analytics company that helped you make wagers on sports events, right?" "Yes, IntualityAI. What about them?" asked Watson.

"Do you think they could predict the perpetrator of this crime?" asked Holmes.

"That's a possibility," mused Watson. "They might be able to provide probabilities for a variety of scenarios. I've been impressed with their accuracy in predicting sports as well as financial markets, opinion polls and health. Do you want me to reach out to them? I believe they are located in North Carolina."

"What do you think Rob?" asked Holmes.

"No harm trying, I guess. But first, I'd like to contact our medical expert, Dr. Pugastan. He told us that he knew of someone in the artificial intelligence field who might be helpful in the investigation. I'd like to find out if he knows anything about this company and this Renier fellow," said Rob.

Rob was quickly on the phone and much to his surprise Dr. Jay answered.

"We are thinking about hiring another outside source that has AI experience in predictions and I wanted to check with you first. Have you ever heard of a company called IntualityAI and their founder Grant Renier? They are based in North Carolina." asked Rob.

"Yes, indeed I have. In fact, he was the very person I was going to suggest if you needed more help. He and his company have done some very good work in adding the human dimension to artificial intelligence," said Dr Jay. "They are excellent at predictions and could be very helpful," he added. "Sorry, Rob I have to go," said Dr. Jay as alarms could be heard in the background.

Rob turned to the others and said, "Dr. Pugastan has indeed heard of them and recommends them highly. Let's do it."

Within the hour, Watson had made contact with the company in North Carolina and was speaking to Grant Renier, the CEO.

Watson introduced himself and mentioned how impressed he was with IntualityAI 's sports predictions. He then explained the current situation and asked whether IntualityAI might be able to help identify the murderer.

"If you have a reliable data stream, we can simply pass it through our system and see what it comes up with," said Renier.

"We don't need to adapt the data stream in any way?" asked Watson.

"Not at all," responded Renier. "We are different in that regard and much more cost-effective. There is no training, or any other programming required. We take your data stream and send it through IntualityAI's predictive analytics programming, and the program does the rest. It projects the data out into 150 points into the future and provides probabilities of events. When an event reaches a high level of probability, an alert is issued. The probabilities are also graphically mapped in a three-dimensional cube, so you can literally see the different odds and where the predictions are strongest and given with the most confidence."

Watson, Holmes, and Dr. Rob were impressed. They all could immediately see the value of this predictive ability in decision making.

Watson appreciated that this technology could definitely help in decision-making, particularly in the medical and health fields.

Measurement was one thing, but prediction quite another. Sure, you can measure someone's blood pressure, but if you could also provide an alert about an impending stroke or heart attack, that would be a massive development. Moreover, Watson could see that in this scenario, the user would not have to do anything. They, and maybe caregivers or practitioners, would be given an alert and instructions on what to do. This could be extremely valuable for older people who are not particularly good at interaction with technology.

Holmes was musing about whether the technology could look back in time, process the data which were then available, and determine

what he thought of as a "post-diction" – an after the fact prediction
that might shed insight into how solutions are made and could be
improved, either in accuracy or speed.

Dr. Rob was fascinated to imagine how the technology could
enhance Noel's own predictive powers. Could such a system
accurately predict the financial markets, or election results, or many
other things that millions of people are engaged in? As he explored
the IntualityAI website, he saw that all of these conjectures were not
only possibilities but already being used successfully.

After their respective musings and some research, the three of them
enthusiastically agreed to engage IntualityAI. Rob set in motion all
the legal requirements and collected the data sets for IntualityAI to
analyze.

Renier had asked for any relevant data that Noel had accumulated
and any specific data about clues and the persons of interest that had
been uncovered.

Within a matter of hours, IntualityAI was generating its predictions
in terms of whether the perpetrator was either a man or a woman. It
had processed the data that Noel had, including details about Nat
and the major persons of interest.

Finally, Renier was on a video call with the investigators and Rob,
showing them the predictions.

Renier showed the Brits a cube, which was the three-dimensional
representation of the probabilities as the data was being processed.

Renier explained that when IntualityAI had decided on a prediction,
the data in the cube produced a high wave, suggesting an actionable
alert signaling a prediction.

"Unfortunately, as you can see, there is no wave, and thus no actionable alert or confident prediction," said Renier, much to the disappointment of the zoom participants.

"IntualityAI is saying that it could be a man or a woman," said Renier.

There was a silence as the participants on the call tried to find something useful in this latest development.

"So, you're saying that there is a 50 percent chance it could be a man or a woman?" asked Holmes.

Renier confirmed Holmes analysis and then added, "Of course, it could be both a man and a woman."

Watson and Holmes shared a disbelieving glance.

"That's an interesting take. Up to this point we have only been considering one perpetrator, but you're right, it could be more than one," said Holmes.

Sherlock clearly wanted to consider this in more detail immediately, and with the discussion over, Rob ended the call with Renier, thanking him for his potentially valuable input and promising to get back to him in due course.

Holmes and Watson excused themselves from Dr. Rob's presence. They left the computer lab and went upstairs to Watson's room to dissect the possibility that both a man and a woman were involved in Nat's murder.

"Okay. We have Shane, Earl, and Rob as the male persons of interest, and Mary, Rue, and potentially Sandra as the female

persons of interest. Let's consider all the possible pairings," said
Holmes.

"There's Shane and Mary, Shane and Rue, Shane and Sandra. Do
any of them make sense?" asked Watson.

Holmes opined that they would need to be able to identify a possible
motive before evaluating the chances of each duo.

"If this was something to do with the organization and the team, then
to me it seems most likely that it would be Shane and Rue. If there
was an organizational issue, Rue would probably need to be involved
somehow. I can't see Shane getting involved with Sandra in
something like this," said Holmes.

"I agree completely," said Watson.

The investigators then considered the next pairings. Earl and Mary,
Earl and Rue, and Earl and Sandra.

Holmes and Watson speculated that given that Earl had misled them
about his relationships with the opposite sex, he potentially could
have been involved with any of the three women. But what would
his motive be?

The investigators agreed that if Earl were to be involved with any of
the three women it would most likely be Mary. However, why such
a relationship would lead to Nat's murder remained completely
vague.

Finally, they considered Rob and his relationships with Mary, Rue,
and Sandra. Here the investigators disagreed. Holmes thought that
Rob and Sandra might have some relationship beyond what seemed

obvious. Watson thought Rob was more likely to have some sort of relationship with Mary.

The thought process had started, though their speculations hadn't got them any closer to finding out who murdered Nat.

"MI6 will be here tomorrow to do more extensive interviews. We will share with them this new possibility of there being both a man and a woman involved, and they can conduct their interrogations accordingly," said Sherlock.

"Are you still convinced that Khang may have something to do with this?" asked Watson.

"I'm not sure we're convinced of anything at this point. However, If Khang were involved in the crime with one of the female suspects, my initial guess is that would be Sandra," said Holmes.

Watson nodded his agreement.

"We'll have to wait and see whether that intensive background check that Dr. Rob and Noel are running on Khang reveals any more information," said Holmes.

"You asked Dr. Rob to run a background check on Khang?" asked a confused Watson.

"I did indeed," replied Holmes. When Watson asked why, Holmes gave a simple reply.

"The more I can distract him and that computer of his with stupid, irrelevant tasks, the more chance I have of winning this particular game," said Holmes succinctly.

"Oh, by the way," added Sherlock, "I have also asked Dr. Rob to research the relationship between murder and belief in heaven. Hopefully that will be another useless distraction and waste of time."

Watson dropped his head into his hands as he now understood why Holmes insisted on asking this question to all the persons of interest.

Holmes then remembered another item, which was of real importance. He reminded Watson that they had to ask Mary Heald what she meant when she said she could explain the money under Nat's bed. They called Dr. Heald and found that she was still actually working in her office and available for a few minutes. They met in the investigator's temporary office.

After the usual pleasantries, Holmes asked the bioengineer whether she recalled telling them that she could explain the money under Nat's bed. Mary nodded in the affirmative and addressed the problem.

"I'm sure you have found in your investigative work that the most bizarre things sometimes end up having the simplest of explanations," Mary started.

"When we were all recruited into this challenging duty, it was clear that this conflict could have major and boundless consequences. Early on we deduced that such consequences could easily lead to the collapse of not just the economy but the entire banking system. All of us thus decided to withdraw a decent amount of money in cash in the event of such a disaster. Apparently, Nat kept his under his bed. Personally, I have chosen a less obvious place for my savings. I hope this information is useful, although we would all appreciate it if you did not make this public knowledge."

Holmes expressed his appreciation for her insight and update.

"As you say, Dr. Heald, sometimes the most perplexing of problems have the simplest solutions," said Holmes. "Thank you for your time."

Then the clock struck ten, signaling the end of a long day. Tomorrow would see the beginning of a new phase of the investigation with the arrival of MI6.

Holmes and Watson retired to their rooms.

Down in the basement, Dr. Rob and Noel were considering the recent conversation with the investigators.

"Noel, we must do much more research into murders like this to find the missing link and solve the problem before Holmes and Watson do. The man is still arrogantly fixed on human intelligence to the detriment of artificial intelligence."

Dr. Rob had already considered some questions to research. He was specifically focused on the profiles of murderers in this situation – the murder of an older gay man by another male who knew him.

Then there was another variable to be explored – the IQ of the killer.

Noel found data from serial killers which showed that high IQ murderers preferred to use bombs, but on the next level down on the IQ scale, average IQ perpetrators use poison and strangulation. Lower IQ killers use brute force or a weapon, either a knife or a gun, or simply bludgeoning their victim to death.

Dr. Rob was fascinated by these data, especially the use of poison. Perhaps he was on to something here?

On further programming, Noel produced some interesting characteristics of serial killers. While Dr. Rob didn't think it was likely that any of his main male suspects were serial killers, he was interested to discover that the main personality characteristics of such murderers were that they had an obsession with power, and were expert manipulators, egotistical braggers, and charmers.

The first person who came to Dr. Rob's mind was Earl, although a moment's reflection suggested that Ron also showed some of these characteristics.

Another analysis by Noel revealed that more than 54 percent of victims knew their killer. Another source suggested that as many as 80 percent not only knew their victims, but some of them knew each other intimately. Dr. Rob once again thought about Nat's homosexuality and its role in the murder. He thought about which suspect in his mind, Earl or Ron, was more likely to have been engaged in that way with Nat.

Rob and Noel then investigated the mental state of murderers. There were the characteristics of serial killers that they had already uncovered but there was also another category that seemed very important.

Noel uncovered data on murderers who killed as a result of a brain injury or trauma. There were some famous cases which intrigued Dr. Rob.

One was the famous killer Charles Whitman, a former Marine who killed 11 people in 1966 from a tower at the University of Texas, after previously murdering his mother and his wife. Whitman was a smart and polite child and at the time was the youngest boy ever to achieve Eagle scout status. Subsequent investigation showed that Whitman had a brain tumor and showed recent changes in his behavior, but this had not been accepted officially as the cause of Whitman's destruction.

Other similar stories suggested a more causal link between brain injury. In one case, a typically well-mannered man threw his wife out of their second-floor apartment window during an argument. The man was found to have a significant brain tumor, with reports of his behavior becoming more aggressive and uncommon over the previous weeks, presumably because of his developing tumor. Rob immediately thought about the recent reports of Ron's increasing moodiness and anger.

In another case a well-respected teacher, who was found to have become uncommonly aggressive and sexual, was found to have a brain tumor. Once it was removed, he returned to his normal, well mannered self. However, a few months later his aggressive behavior resumed, at which point doctors found that his tumor had returned.

Further research suggested that about 9 percent of violence or crime could be directly attributed to traumatic brain injury, and 14 percent were associated with frontal lobe injury. Noel found one 2014 study which found that as many as 50 of 249 mass murder cases could be attributed to a head injury.

Rob did not doubt that brain trauma or injury could unquestionably influence people's thoughts, feelings, and moral connection. He then asked himself the obvious question, did anyone on the team, but specifically Earl or Ron, display recent changes in their behavior?

Had anyone on the team ever shown the egotism, obsession with power, and manipulation that seemed to characterize some killers?

Rob believed that the answers to these critical questions, were the keys to solving the mystery and reveal the identity of Nat's murderer.

Rob was determined to keep exploring these characteristics that would ultimately lead him and Noel to unveiling the perpetrator. However, time was of the essence. Holmes needed to be beaten to the finishing line.

He decided that Noel needed to interview the persons of interest and ask them these important questions, and do so soon.

Chapter Seventeen

Thursday: 8:00am

"The will to survive is not as important as the will to prevail ...the answer to criminal aggression is retaliation."
Jeff Cooper

The next morning everyone was summoned by Shane and Ron to meet in the conference room before breakfast. The MI6 team had yet to arrive, but they had very important information.

"MI6 isn't here yet, why are they calling us down? Rob asked.

"I don't know, maybe they've narrowed down the suspect list," Mary said.

Holmes and Watson joined the team and Ron began the briefing.

"There have been two drone attacks on military AI facilities in the past twelve hours. One was in Germany and the other in North Carolina. Most of the drones were shot down or otherwise repelled, but in North Carolina, there was a significant fire, and several people were injured and taken to hospital. The alert status here, and in every other facility, has been raised to the maximum level. The security here at Bletchley has been increased around the facility and in the area, generally. Just be on high alert and respond immediately when, and if, the alarm siren sounds."

"As you all know, the MI6 team will be arriving shortly. The two people you will interact with mostly are Jim Faulkner and Dr.

Colleen Wilson. They will be investigating the scene and, of course, talking with each of you."

The team immediately started murmuring to each other.

"Please, let us not be attacked," said Rue to Ron.

"I wouldn't rule it out," replied Ron.

"Well, if that does happen, we will all be together in the bunker. It might even be fun," Earl said winking at Mary.

"Rob, you'll have to leave your machines alone and hang out with us," said Rue.

"That's what I am afraid of," he replied. "But, of course, that's the reason we put most of the big technology underground."

"Ok, people, let's catch up with the rest of the news," said Shane trying to end the speculation.

There then followed the usual morning briefing. There had been more success in forcing Chinese forces back in Taiwan but on the other hand the conflict was taking a massive toll on the world economy and being equally destructive for both sides of the conflict. There were hopes that this scenario of collapse would force both sides to seek an end to the conflict as soon as possible. But at that moment, it seemed that this was a mere desperate hope than an imminent reality.

As the meeting ended, Rob approached Holmes with an update on Noel's research on Khang. He took Sherlock and Watson aside and gave them the update.

"We have processed masses of data, trying to track Khang's heritage and possible connections in China. We have turned up some interesting things," said Rob.

"Khang's parents left China more than forty years ago. However, they came from a family that was very committed to the Chinese regime. There's evidence that many of the family were very militant and actively involved in supporting the Chinese government. We can't find any direct ties between Khang's parents and those supporters, but that doesn't mean they weren't part of that group. Perhaps that's why they left and came to the UK. In any event, it does appear that some of Khang's relatives, distant cousins, are still actively involved in Chinese operations, and are likely to be active in this conflict. At the moment, we have found no evidence that Khang's immediate family here in England are doing anything illegal, but we're still tracking that data down."

Watson was impressed by Noel's ability to find this information. He was certainly aware that it would have taken mere humans much longer, if ever, to reveal such a possible connection. The question now, however, was what did this information really mean?

Holmes on the other hand was thinking of other irrelevant questions that would significantly occupy Dr. Rob and Noel and keep them from pursuing meaningful leads. As he thought about it, another idea came to mind. What was the relationship between dominant hand and murder? He knew that the only left hander on the team and a person of interest was Earl, but because Earl was one of Dr. Rob's leading suspects, he and Noel would likely be lured into spending valuable time researching this futile topic.

"Dr. Rob, I had a very interesting insight today. I think it would be most valuable if you could have Noel do some comprehensive research on the relationship between hand dominance and murder. What per centage of murderers are left-handed?" said Holmes.

Dr. Rob was indeed intrigued.

"That's an excellent point, Holmes. We'll dig into that data right away," said Rob. "By the way, Noel has created a list of questions related to the critical variables we were discussing, and we hope to interview everyone very soon."

"Sounds interesting," said Watson. "We'll check in with you and see what you find."

Chapter Eighteen

Thursday: Noon

"By the way, the point between rationality and what we would call the irrational is a very difficult point to establish. There's no specific line, as you know."
Leo Ornstein

With her initial interviews with the subjects almost complete, Colleen sat down to discuss things with Jim, Sherlock, and Watson.

"I'm not getting much, if anything, on the possible existence of any male-female romantic relationships, let alone what they would say about possible motives," said the tall, blonde psychologist. "Honestly, I'm not picking anything up at all. Sure, Earl can be a bit flirtatious, especially with Mary, but I am not getting anything more than that. I don't see Shane, Rob, or Rue being involved in anything like that either. Perhaps the implication that there were two culprits is misleading us?"

There was a silence.

"What did this Renier fellow say about the prediction, again?" asked Colleen.

"He said that the prediction in this case was a fifty/fifty chance the perpetrator was a man or a woman," said Watson.

"Wait a minute!" said Sherlock excitedly. "Perhaps we have misunderstood that prediction."

The others looked at Holmes in bewilderment.

"Perhaps the prediction that it was 50 percent a man and 50 percent a woman doesn't mean we should be looking for a couple but rather we should be looking for a transgender person!" exclaimed Holmes.

"You have a point there, Sherlock!" said Colleen. Jim seemed to agree, but Watson was less than enthusiastic. He assumed that this was another of Sherlock's diversionary, time-wasting tactics designed to distract Rob and Noel.

"Do we have any evidence that any of our suspects is transgender?" asked Jim.

"None whatsoever," said Colleen before adding, "At the moment."

Holmes paused and recalled his conversation with Mary Heald, a stunning woman who had never been married and revealed very little interest in men. He immediately made a note to ask Rob and Noel to explore the history of the seven persons of interest, with specific reference to any gender issues.

"Did you conduct your interviews with possible gender issues in mind, Colleen?" asked Holmes.

"No, not really. But they were just the start, more like general discussion. Obviously, I was planning on doing more intensive examination. Not just trying to get information, but dive deeper," suggested Colleen. "Now it looks like I'll have to dive deeper than I originally thought."

"Hypnosis?" asked Jim.

Colleen nodded in the affirmative.

Sherlock and Watson inquired about such use of hypnosis.

"Well, let's see what Chat GPT and Noel say about this matter," suggested Colleen.

Within a minute she was reading the description given by the computer about forensic hypnosis.

"Hypnosis has been occasionally used in criminal investigations and interviews as a tool to enhance memory recall and gather information from witnesses or suspects. However, it's important to note that the use of hypnosis in this context is controversial and has limitations. Here are some key points to consider:

"Hypnosis and memory: Hypnosis aims to induce a trance-like state where the individual is highly focused and receptive to suggestions. Proponents argue that hypnosis can help unlock repressed memories or enhance recall of forgotten details. However, the validity and accuracy of these memories remain subject to debate, as hypnosis can also lead to the creation of false memories.

"Admissibility in court: The use of hypnotically induced statements as evidence varies across jurisdictions. Many legal systems have strict rules regarding the admissibility of evidence obtained through hypnosis, recognizing the potential for suggestibility, false memories, and the lack of scientific consensus on its reliability.

"Ethical considerations: Hypnosis involves a power dynamic between the hypnotist and the subject, which raises ethical concerns. Coercion, leading questions, or unintentional suggestions from the interviewer can influence the subject's responses. To minimize these risks, only trained professionals experienced in forensic hypnosis should conduct the interviews.

"Alternative methods: Hypnosis is not the only technique available for eliciting information in criminal interviews. Established methods like cognitive interviewing, which focuses on enhancing memory recall through non-hypnotic means, are generally considered more reliable and scientifically validated.

Jim and Colleen agreed that the short description was pretty accurate.

"Colleen is an expert in forensic hypnosis," affirmed Jim.

Watson wondered whether any of the persons of interest would refuse to cooperate and what that would imply, but Colleen quickly reassured him that they wouldn't realize the nature of the session unless a serious issue was revealed.

Both Holmes and Watson knew about hypnosis and had a general understanding of the way it is conducted. They asked Colleen how she carries out a typical session.

"It depends on the purpose and circumstances. For the most part it is not deep hypnosis, but more of a communication style to get beyond the interviewee's cognitive defenses. Sometimes it can go much deeper, though, if the interviewee gets immersed into it and the subconscious appears. Ideally, we want the subconscious to take over, because it rarely lies, or manipulates the truth."

Colleen continued, "The subconscious is about feelings, not facts. Its language is emotions, not words. It speaks in feelings and images. It's the world at its most fundamental level. It's all about experience, not description. It's the world of raw feelings unadulterated by language, logic, or any attempt at comprehension. It's the basis of our lives."

"Now, I need to clarify something for you that can often be misunderstood about the subconscious," continued Colleen. "The best metaphor is that of an iceberg. Imagine an iceberg where there is a small amount of the ice showing above the water. That is consciousness. Then below the surface is what is not in conscious, the majority of the iceberg."

"Now just below the surface are things that can easily come into view. Freud called this the 'preconscious,' which are anything from feelings to ideas that exist. They are below the surface but can be recalled at any time. These could be memories or even ideas and beliefs, that we don't constantly think about, but lurk just below the surface of consciousness and can be easily recalled. However, some things, like beliefs, live just below the surface and influence us even if we don't consciously interact or analyze them. This is the bases of the so-called biases."

"The further down the iceberg something goes, like a memory, the more difficult it is to re-enter consciousness. This is where and how traumatic memories are repressed. They live at the bottom of the iceberg."

Both the investigators were impressed by Dr. Colleen's vivid description of the subconscious. And without knowing it both Watson and Holmes were musing about what Dr. Rob and Noel would say about the subconscious.

Could AI access the subconscious of others? How would it interpret such vague information? How could it connect the vagaries of subconscious "information" and make sense of it? Would a robot need its own version of the subconscious to fully understand it and what any subconscious material might mean?

Both Holmes and Watson understood that this question was at the heart of the issues surrounding robotic capabilities and limits. With the right instruction and training a robot could, theoretically, create anything from an amazing copy of the Mona Lisa to an atomic bomb. But without such training, what could it do? And would such training involve only copying motor movements, or would it involve subconscious processes? The ability to feel, sentience, and the subconscious seemed to be at the heart of the question about the limits of artificial intelligence.

This seemed key to both Watson and Holmes because feelings seemed to be at the heart of morality as well as the subconscious. Without feelings, there is no morality. Without feelings, whether you can kill 3,000 people or save them is simply a matter of logistics. Without feelings, the only thing that matters is capability. Without feelings, there is no purpose. Without feelings, you are just a psychopath. You might be very capable, very smart, very rational, but you're still a psychopath.

As the meeting ended, Holmes was about to leave when he turned to Colleen and Jim.

"I'd be very interested in how your hypnosis goes with one particular person of interest. I'll catch up later and tell you to whom I am referring."

Then Holmes made his way down to Dr. Rob's laboratory and the home of Noel.

Holmes explained that he had rethought some of the issues and wanted to know if Noel could help with some questions he had.

Dr. Rob asked Sherlock what he was looking for.

"There's the possibility that the perpetrator in this crime is transgender. Is it possible for Noel to search whatever data is relevant and see if he can reveal any relationship between our possible persons of interest and their gender orientation?"

Dr. Rob reflected on the question. He reasoned he could seek as much data as possible about the persons of interest that was available but couldn't make any promises that such a comprehensive search would reveal anything.

"I know it's a long shot, but Noel impressed me with his background search of Khang, and I think this would be worth doing," said Holmes.

Rob assured him he would get on it right away.

Within a few hours, Noel had found something of interest, though its relevance remained completely unclear. Through numerous searches, Noel had uncovered some old photos of Mary in a school play. These seemed to indicate that she was about thirteen at the time. She was the star of the cast, featured in this school promotion of the drama production. There was one strange aspect to the photo. It was clear that Mary was playing the lead role, who was – a man.

Nothing else was discovered, but the photo did engage Rob's curiosity. Was she playing the lead role because she was the best actor, or was something else behind her appearance?

Chapter Nineteen

Thursday: 2:00pm

"The only real valuable thing is intuition."
Albert Einstein

Watson and Holmes discussed the case over a late lunch.

"What's driving your sense that the killer is a woman?"

"That's a very good question, Watson. I've been trying to figure that out myself. I guess if I knew what it was, it would become less of an intuition and more of a fact, or utterly useless."

"Is it something about the crime scene?" asked Watson.

"I don't think so, but we should go back in there and see if anything resonates."

"Yes, we should. Or perhaps is there some unarticulated connection from a previous case?" suggested Watson.

"I've been wondering that. Nothing is coming. Can you think of any possible similarities to any of our previous cases?"

Watson shook his head. Then continued, "Is it anything to do with any of the female suspects?"

"I think it might be, but again it's all so damn vague. There's one of them that, I don't know, makes me suspicious. I can't identify why, and I certainly can't trust it, not yet anyway."

"Do you mind telling me which lady this is?" asked Watson, despite already knowing what Holmes' reply would be.

"No, Watson, you know I'm not going to tell you. Once we, or anyone else, starts limiting the scope of the investigation, we're going down the rabbit hole. The anchoring bias, and all that. If I gain more insight and the timing is right, then, of course, I will reveal who it is."

Watson nodded knowingly. He didn't expect Holmes to tell him who it was.

"Let's go back to Nat's room and see if that enlightens me further," said Holmes.

After unlocking the door to the crime scene, Holmes and Watson began their re-examination, but this time they were looking more for sensations rather than facts. This is a skill that Holmes, in particular, had mastered. It was one thing to look at a crime scene specifically looking for clues, it was another to simply experience the environment. That was the secret of looking beyond the obvious, the materialistic, the preconceived. This had had helped Holmes numerous times by sensing evidence when it could not be found. Sensory human intelligence.

Both of them inhaled the air of the dead man's room. It was probably now too late to detect any smell that may have had significance, like lingering perfume or deodorant. They hadn't consciously detected anything during their initial investigation, and this inhalation was no different, just the stale air of death.

They had already looked for footprints, but none were obvious on the wooden flooring or glorious rugs. Footprints are often a critical clue, providing a good estimate of the weight and gait of the perpetrator. Holmes got onto his hands and knees to examine the carpet, and while doing so looked under the bed once again. Even the smallest detail, like for example, a fastener of an earring, could make a massive difference, but again, nothing was found.

"My gut is still telling me it's a woman," said Holmes.

"Perhaps you need an antacid?" quipped Dr. Watson with uncharacteristic sarcasm.

"No, I don't think so Watson, but I certainly understand that the feeling in your stomach can be due to something you have eaten, or something that's eating you."

They stayed in the room a little while longer, continuing to seek out the source of the Holmes' intuition.

"Perhaps it's nothing to do with this scene, and more to do with the people themselves," offered Watson more constructively.

"I think you might be right about that," agreed Holmes. "We need to talk to these three women again."

"Actually," said Watson, "I wonder whether Colleen couldn't help loosen this feeling from the grip of your subconscious. Perhaps some of that forensic hypnosis could help clarify your thoughts?"

"Thanks for reminding me Watson. I was going to talk to her about this. I don't think I need to be hypnotized, but you're right. Colleen seems like a very smart woman and knowledgeable in these matters. I think I will indeed seek a conversation with her and see if she can help unravel this intuition," said Holmes.

In the meantime, Noel and Rob started their interviews with their four main persons of interest: Mary, Rue, Earl and Ron.

Chapter Twenty

Friday: 11:00am

"The two operations of our understanding, intuition and deduction, on which alone we have said we must rely in the acquisition of knowledge."
Rene Descartes

Over the previous two days, Noel had interviewed all the persons of interest. Noel had compiled a list of questions that he thought would be very critical in identifying the major suspect and ultimately the perpetrator.

Some of the questions were very direct and elicited different perceptions and responses from the interviewees.

For example, when Mary was asked question number 8, the conversation went like this.

Noel: *Have you ever killed someone?*

Mary: Not yet.

However, with Ron the scenario was different.

Noel: *Have you ever killed someone?*
Ron: Yes, I have.

Noel: *What were the circumstances?*

Ron: I was on military duty in Afghanistan.

Noel: *What happened?*

Ron: Our position was attacked by terrorists. Fortunately, we were prepared and were able to blast the attackers with many rounds of ammunition which killed most of them.

Noel: *How many did you kill?*

Ron: Can't be sure because we were all shooting, but I know I killed one of them and probably contributed to the deaths of at least one other, if not more.

Noel: *Are you sorry that you killed someone?*

Ron: No, not really. Sorry that I had to kill someone but not sorry for causing the death of someone who wanted to kill me.

There were some questions that were answered in the affirmative by the majority , if not all of the persons of interest.

For example, in answer to question 5, Have you ever been depressed?, Rue, Mary, Earl and Ron all answered that they had been depressed at one point or another. And they all confided that they had been on anti-depressant medication at one point or another.

However, it was Ron and Earl whose responses were of most interest and significance to Noel and of course, Rob.

In addition to the admission of killing someone, Ron also endorsed some questions that elicited more suspicion.

Noel asked Ron Question 3 which was *"Do you know much about poisons?"*

"Actually I do," admitted Ron. "When I was getting my Masters degree I wrote my thesis on the use of poisons in suicide and murder."

What did you conclude? asked Noel.

"In murder cases, poisons have often been favored due to their discreet nature, which can make them difficult to detect," said Ron. "Suicide involving poisons often reflects deeply personal struggles, mental health issues, or extreme circumstances. Individuals may choose poison as a means of ending their lives due to its perceived reliability or as a way to avoid pain and suffering."

That's very interesting responded Noel.

Ron also endorsed another question that Noel considered important.

Have you increased an existing medication or started a new one in the last six months?

"Actually I have. A few months back my doctor noticed my blood pressure was untypically high and he put me on some medications to control it," said Ron.

Did you have any other symptoms?

"Yes, I found myself getting short-tempered very easily."

Have you had a recent brain scan?

"No!" said Ron getting increasingly irked by Noel's questioning. "I don't need a bloody brain scan! By the way, when was the last time you had a damned brain scan!"

What's your sleep like generally? Asked Noel disregarding Ron's tirade.

"Generally it's okay," Ron replied before venting his anger further. "Have you finished with your damned questions!?" Ron blurted out aggressively.

Why do you think that your blood pressure went up so much?

"Because I had to keep addressing the same dumb questions from people and machines like you!"

Finally, if you had to chose one of your colleagues as Nat's murderer, who would it be?

"I'm very suspicious of Earl. He is very smart but also moody. His demeanor can change in a heartbeat, which suggests to me he can be very impulsive. OK, well now I have told you who did it, can I leave?" asked Ron sarcastically.

I have all I need for now. So, yes, you may leave.

"Thank God!" said Ron as he stomped out of the room.

Given Ron's albeit snarky testimony, Rob and Noel also had their suspicions of Earl which were at the forefront during their interview with him.

Earl's notorious difficulty with sleeping, mood changes and sometimes inappropriate interactions with the women at the Range, as well as his admitted depression and medication use, portrayed someone who was potentially capable of committing something as drastic as murder.

Noel's questions were mostly focused on these areas of interest when interviewing Earl.

Have you had sex with anyone on the team?

"Excuse me?" said Earl, taken back by the direct nature of the question.

Have you had sex with Mary, Rue or any other women here at the Range?

"I'm not answering that absurd question!" responded Earl.

Why not?

"Because it's none of your business!" roared Earl. "And what has that got to do with Nat's death?"

Well, that's what I am trying to explore, Dr. Earl. So, I would appreciate a direct answer.

"No, I have not had sex with any of the women here at the Range."

Have you had sex with any of the women outside of the Range?

"NO!" roared Earl before adding, "Have you had sex with anyone, ever?"

I will not answer that question.

What were you doing the night that Nat died?

"I was sleeping in my room," replied before adding "On my own."

But your sleep is notoriously bad. Did you wake up at all that night?

"I don't remember," said Earl dismissively.

What do you typically do when you wake up at night?

"Try to go back to sleep. If I can't I will try to read or meditate."

Did you hear anything unusual the night that Nat died? Your room is close to his is it not?

"Yes, but I do not recall hearing anything at all. Now, remember my sleep is usually good in the early part of the evening. That's when I'm likely to be in deep sleep. It's the middle of the night when I typically wake up and have difficulty dropping off again."

Who do you think did this to Nat?

"To be honest, I suspect that you had something to do with it," said Earl.

What exactly do you think that I did?

"Possibly brainwashed him with fake news which made Nat want to kill himself," said Earl resolutely.

How would I do that?

"Probably through some social media account. We all know that Nat could be a bit fixated on his social media feeds. It would be easy for you to bombard him with negative messaging about the massively deadly impact of his actions."

Thank you, Dr. Earl, that will be all for now.

"Yes, I bet it is," said Earl.

After Earl had left, Rob and Noel discussed the implications of their interviews.

"Well, we are certain that it is a man, Noel," said Rob.

Yes, indeed. We know it was neither you nor Shane, which leaves only two possibilities, Earl or Ron.

Rob asked "Who do you think it is?"

Earl obviously has some mood issues and can be very impulsive. His relationship with women and how that might have impacted his feelings towards Nat is a question that needs answering.

"I am still having difficulty seeing how that has anything to do with Nat unless there are things that we are missing. Personally, I don't see it," said Rob.

Which leaves us with Ron. Let's not forget that he left the Range without permission soon after Nat's body was found. And he also has a recent history of mood changes and anger which I think is significant.

"Absolutely, Noel. He reminds me so much of those stories told by neuro-criminologists   which tell of people showing a significant change in their behavior in the weeks before committing a crime."

Most people have noticed this about Ron and he even admitted himself that he needed to get medication to calm himself down. I am speculating he has some kind of brain tumor that stimulated violent action towards Nat. And let's not forget he has admitted to murder in the past and knows a lot about poisons.

"Outstanding, Noel. I think we have figured this mystery out and done so before Holmes has! Well done! But, let's just keep this to ourselves for now and keep Sherlock diving down the wrong hole."

Chapter Twenty-One

Friday: 1:30pm

"Conflict is the beginning of consciousness."
M. Esther Harding

It was time for Colleen to start her next round of interviews. She hoped these would be more revealing. It was forensic hypnosis time.

Colleen based the timing of her interviews merely on the availability of the members of the team. Earl was the first to participate.

Colleen welcomed Earl into her temporary office, which was perfect for the type of interview she had in mind. There were no windows, and she had turned the light down fairly low, so it barely cast shadows on the wall. It was the shadows in the interviewee's consciousness that she was trying to capture.

"How is it going today?" Colleen opened vaguely.

"Well, we are working on something that could be very important, so it's been quite stimulating," said Earl, eyeing Colleen's blonde hair.

"Surely almost everything you do here is of the utmost importance. You must feel a tremendous sense of purpose working in this context?" said Colleen.

Colleen copied Earl's smile, and as he sat back in his chair, she did the same.

"Well, I don't think about that much. I think we are all too immersed in the details to see the big picture most of the time. It's only when something big happens, like Nat's success in luring the Chinese, that the true significance of what we're doing is brought home," said Earl. "But I do appreciate the significance of the operation and am very proud to be part of this team. There are only a few people who could work as successfully as we do. But yes, it is a sacrifice."

"It must be difficult to relax in such an atmosphere."

"Yes, I have always had a bit of a problem sleeping, and this context doesn't help."

Colleen asked what measures Earl took in order to help him get to sleep.

"I don't like medication if I can avoid it. I lose count of sheep, so that doesn't work," Earl said with a smirk. "And some of my best ideas come while in that semi-drowsy state. More recently I have been trying an AVE device and that has helped more than I thought."

Colleen confirmed that Earl was referencing Audio Visual Entrainment, which is delivered by a device sending different audio-visual stimuli, generally in the form of light and sound frequencies, to the different sides of the brain.

"I would think with your musical expertise, sound and music would definitely help you relax, for sure," said Colleen. "And I have had several clients who have tried AVE and said that it helped them enormously. One client reminds me of you, and her sleeping has really improved, so I definitely would recommend you keep using it. Like this client, you will find that one day you will be sleeping like a baby."

"Thanks, that's valuable encouragement," smiled Earl.

Colleen then switched the conversation to the difficult parts of Earl's life.

"I see that life has not been easy for you, Earl. You have an autistic son, right?"

Earl paused and looked down at the floor.

"Yes," he said slowly, "that might be the most challenging aspect of my life."

Another pause.

Colleen spoke.

"I know how difficult that can be. My sister-in-law has a son on the autistic spectrum."

Earl responded, "I always imagined that I would be able to teach my children about the wonders of nature and science and music, and all the amazing things that I have experienced. That they would achieve great things in the world, especially in science. But, sadly, that has not been the case. Johnathan is in his own way a smart young man, but no one can understand him. He has an amazing memory, but uses it to store irrelevant facts, like the members of rock bands and their birthdays. It is frustrating because I love him but don't know how to convey that to him in a way that he understands."

Earl's face showed an uncharacteristic grimace, as if someone had punched him in the gut.

"It's a tragedy that I feel I have no control over," said Earl, beginning to tear up. "And I hate it when I don't have control."

"I have worked with several people like Johnathan," said Colleen. "And I have found that they have all one amazing characteristic."

Earl looked up at Colleen through his tearful eyes, wanting to know what the characteristic was.

"The neurodiverse, the disabled, the different, they all share one thing," Colleen paused deliberately to get Earl to wonder what that characteristic was.

When a few seconds had passed, Colleen continued.

"They challenge all of us. They take us out of our normal perceptions. They are 'God's Secret Shoppers.' They call on us to understand, to empathize, to relate when it is seemingly difficult to do so. Just like many disabled people, they are the outsiders that test out moral compass. Our ability to feel compassion, gratitude, humility, and even love."

Earl started to cry harder.

"I am so frustrated that I cannot change him and make him happier and more successful, productive," he blurted out tearfully.

"You love him, I can see that. And that's the main thing," said Colleen. "Perhaps it's not your job to change him or cast him in the mold that you think is success."

Earl looked up and silently acknowledged Colleen's kindness and wisdom.

Colleen knew to pause her side of the conversation and allow Earl's emotional state to reveal more of his subconscious.

His emotional expression didn't change. If anything, it became more pronounced as sadness and guilt once more etched themselves on his countenance.

Eventually he spoke.

"And then there's Susan."

Colleen clarified that he was talking about his first wife, the mother of Johnathan. Then she knew to shut up.

There was another pause as Earl's often hidden thoughts and feelings surfaced. His subconscious began to emerge in the dark light of the office.

Earl sighed deeply.

"After the initial phase of love and attraction faded away, it was an effort to keep the relationship going. I'm sure we had different love languages. You are, of course, familiar with that book?" asked Earl.

Colleen acknowledged that Earl was referring to the classic book *The Five Love Languages* by Gary Chapman.

"We just didn't connect at all." Earl started to sob openly and hard.

After a long pause, Colleen prompted Earl once more.

"Perhaps there were other reasons?" suggested Colleen.

"Maybe. I thought because of our similar scientific interests we would be a great match, but it didn't work out that way. In fact, more often than not we would argue about the subject. Our common interest turned out to be more divisive than unifying."

Colleen confirmed that Earl and Susan had divorced after eight years.

"Yes," said Earl sadly. "We had enough of our disagreements. And then you know how it goes. The communication gets more and more angry and divisive and leads down the road to the lawyer's office. And then you have really entered the binary world of the legal system and the family court, from which there's no escape," Earl sniffed loudly.

Colleen paused to allow Earl to process the feelings. The bright, mercurial, brilliant star of a man had been temporarily transformed into an old asteroid, hurtling through nowhere, lost and alone. Colleen did not want him to fall into the black hole of repression, the bottom of the iceberg. The black hole of the subconscious, where dark matters are stored and can only break the massive gravitational pull of avoidance when there's a quantum burst of energy that can reveal the truth.

"I'm sure you must have had fun at times, being a famous, single professor at a world-renowned educational institution?" Colleen said, almost poetically, trying to change the tone.

A semi-smile returned as the asteroid avoided the emotional black hole.

"Yes, I had some fun times," said Earl before pausing as memories of several of the young girls and women he had dated, flashed into his mind.

"And then I met Ella, the love of my life."

Colleen asked how Earl and Ella had met.

"We met at a conference in London. We hit it off immediately. I was a little older than she was and was still very much immersed in my career. She tolerated that, perhaps more than she had to. Also, her parents could be overbearing and would insist on visiting us for days at a time. That's when I developed my Theory of Relatives."

Colleen shot an enquiring look.

"The Theory of Relatives states that when family come to visit, time lengthens and space shortens," explained Earl.

Colleen laughed out loud, but Earl's emotions were going in the opposite direction.

"I was devastated when she died."

Earl's face dropped as his eyes started tearing up again. If this was a yoga position it would be called "sad dog."

More guilt and sadness erupted from Earl's volcanic spirit as he talked about Ella's cardiovascular disease and untimely death.

"If I loved her more, perhaps her heart would have been stronger," said Earl tragically.

"Or if you loved her less, she might have died sooner," said Colleen.

At this point Colleen had gotten a decent picture of Earl and some of his most critical issues. He certainly was a genius, but below the glittering surface of brilliance was a man dogged by guilt and regret, possible victims of a male mentality that assumed perfection and success were not negotiable.He had a history of numerous relationships, an area of his life where his boundaries were probably too lax, where perhaps his ego became too dominant.

Colleen thanked him for his time and said she would be available if Earl wanted to talk more, and that indeed she might want to follow up with him.

Earl, stood up, flashed a warm smile, and thanked Colleen for her time. Colleen noted how quickly Earl's outward persona was able to change, oscillating rapidly between glossy charm and soulful guilt.

After Earl left, Colleen added to her notes.

"Is E bipolar?" she wrote at the bottom of the page.

Before her next appointment with Rue, Colleen went to meet Sherlock to see if she could help him understand more about his intuition.

Colleen invited Holmes into her office. He had asked to see her for help with his intuitive feeling about one of the suspects and she willingly agreed to see him.

"How's it going today, my dear Sherlock?" the psychologist asked.

"I'm still trying to plough through the evidence, but as I mentioned to you, I have an intuitive feeling about one of the persons of interest. For the life of me, I can't identify where this feeling is coming from or what lies behind it. I think it could be extremely helpful if I could identify what my gut is trying to tell me," said Sherlock. "I am hoping you can help."

"Well, let's see. Can you tell me who this concerns?"

Sherlock paused while his natural inhibition about revealing his thoughts before they have been confirmed kicked in. Eventually he worked himself up to reveal who he was talking about.

"I think you know already. It's Rue, of course." he said succinctly.

"So, you have some intuitive feeling about Rue but can't accurately identify where this feeling is coming from or what it is about, right?" asked Colleen.

Holmes nodded in the affirmative.

"Well, as I am sure you know, intuition can be incredibly revealing and accurate, or simply irrelevant and misguided. Do you use intuition a lot in your work?" asked Colleen.

"Quite a lot. I believe that intuition is a reflection of one's experience, and as such can be very helpful, especially in criminal investigations. Experience is critical, perhaps more so than compelling logic. Your experience is a collection of all of those things that have worked and have not worked, and as a result is a tremendous guide to the practical knowledge that you have both consciously and subconsciously. It's the encyclopedia of your practical knowledge. The problem is that when it is subconscious you have to figure out what your body, and mind, are trying to tell you," said Sherlock.

"Okay, I understand. So, tell me about your impression of Rue," started Colleen.

"Well, I see that she is a very focused woman. Almost too focused. I talked to Dr Shane about this, and he agreed. He explained about the different parts of the brain and the salience network that switches you from a relaxed state to a focused one. When you have difficulty switching into a focused state you might well be diagnosed with attention deficit disorder, but Rue displays the exact opposite. She's hypervigilant," said Holmes.

"What are the implications of that?" asked the psychologist.

"Well, for one thing, it suggests to me that she might be hiding something. It's like she's always on the defense." Holmes paused for a moment before continuing. "Actually, that's helpful. I hadn't quite articulated it that way before," he pondered before continuing. "She seems very defensive to me. Perhaps that's what I am sensing. I had been viewing her incredible focus as a positive trait, but I now see that it could be hiding something a lot more negative."

"Does she remind you of anyone else you have known either in your personal life or in the course of your career?"

Holmes thought for quite a while, scanning his memory.

"Nothing is resonating there. No-one in particular. I do believe that it is her defensiveness that I'm picking up. And I do know that there's always a reason why people are defensive. So, naturally, defensive people make me suspicious about what they are hiding and why. Sometimes, in fact more often than not, that defensiveness is ultimately revealing. How are you progressing in your interviews with her?"

"I'm still working on it. I think I am getting closer, but we will see what happens eventually and whether it has any relevance to the crime," said Colleen.

And with that, the conversation ended. and Holmes left the room a little more enlightened than when he entered. It helped to talk things out, and getting a different perspective than Watson's was valuable in this instance.

Once the door closed Colleen mused about Sherlock's intuition. She had a similar feeling about Rue.

Chapter Twenty-Two

Friday: 3:00pm

*"Thinking is the hardest work there is, which is
probably the reason why so few engage in it."*
Henry Ford

It was time for Colleen to interview Rue again. She reflected on their last meeting as she listened to the heavy patter of rain rattling against the windows, but that noise faded as the women entered the windowless office.

"How can I help you today, Dr. Wilson?" asked Rue as she took her seat opposite the psychologist.

"Well, I just want to go over some personal things. No doubt Earl and Mary have mentioned their recent conversations with me," said Colleen.

"No, they haven't said anything at all," admitted Rue.

"Well, please understand that this more detailed discussion is really about trying to identify any clues that might help us in solving this matter. There may be things that you know, or you haven't really thought about, that might be useful to the investigation," said Colleen.

"Well, I'm happy to tell you anything that I can that will help, especially about Nat," said Rue.

Colleen asked Rue about her impression of Nat.

"He was a great guy. He followed all the rules and went about his work so diligently. He was smart, and caring. From an admin's point of view, he was a great worker and the ideal teammate. He did everything that was required and then some. I knew I could always rely on him."

Colleen then asked whether Rue recalled any special requests that Nat had.

"I don't believe so. As I said, he was the ideal worker and teammate."

"Did you spend much time with him after hours, outside work?"

"Not really. I personally believe that we all have to sustain professional boundaries for many reasons, not least of which is the importance and priority of this mission," Rue replied sincerely.

Colleen pondered about Rue's use of the word "really." She explored further.

"Have you ever been in Nat's room?"

Rue looked a little dismayed by the possible implication of the question.

"Well, I have never been in there alone with him, if that's what you mean," said Rue firmly. "I have been part of security checks with the guards in his room and that sort of thing, but no, I was never alone with him in his room. Or my room, come to that," Rue added anticipating Colleen's next question.

Colleen wanted to break Rue out of her bureaucratic stoicism, a presentation that had always characterized a dispassionate administrator. Why the unbending presentation? Colleen wondered.

"You must have been devastated when you saw Nat's body lying motionless when you and Ron entered the room on that fateful morning."

"I couldn't really comprehend it. Why? Why Nat? Why would someone want to harm him? It was overwhelming," said Rue.

Colleen commented that several of the team members still believed it was a matter of suicide, and asked Rue for her opinion.

"Yes, suicide definitely makes more sense to me," Rue paused. "Much more sense."

"Why do you say that?"

Rue sat back in her chair, pondering the question.

"He could be very down on himself at times. That was very frustrating for all of us to observe." Rue's expression went from administratively neutral to more realistically solemn.

"Do you think he was depressed?"

"Well, you'd probably know that better than I do," suggested Rue. "Come on Rue," said Colleen stepping up the stakes, "You know about depression. You have had some very tough times and must have experienced it, quite deeply at times, I suspect."

"Well, honestly, I don't like to talk about that part of my life very much. Or even talk about it at all," said Rue defensively.

"I understand. I'm just trying to get your perception of Nat's mood, as someone who knows what deep depression really is," said Colleen pushing the boundaries of the conversation.

"Do I think that Nat was depressed at times? Yes, absolutely. But I don't think it interfered with his work," said Rue.

Well at least Rue didn't deny her own "deep depression," thought Colleen.

"When your depression was at its worst, or very bad, how did you cope?"

Rue thought long and hard how to answer.

"Medications helped, of course. I also tried to find something to focus on; just do something. And perhaps, physical exercise was the most important," Rue said slowly.

"You have had some serious challenges, Rue," said Colleen, trying to capture the moment of Rue's introspection and harness it.

Rue fell silent as Colleen waited.

"Losing your sister must have been terrible. I don't know how I would even cope with something like that," said Colleen.

Gradually, Rue's face and her very soul turned blank. She looked up and stared past Colleen into the colorless wall behind the psychologist.

Colleen noticed Rue's motionless eyes. Her posture had become static. It was like she was stuck in a time warp.

Colleen waited and just observed Rue's frozen persona.

"Rue. Rue can you hear me?" said Colleen.

There was no reply.

"Rue, dear. Can you hear me?" Colleen repeated.

And then it happened.

A wailing siren crashed into the room.

"Oh, my God!" said Colleen. She reached over to Rue and shook her hard, then pulled her up out of the chair. "Rue, we have to leave! Now!"

Suddenly, Rue woke from wherever she had been and returned hyper aroused to the unpleasant reality of an impending attack.

"Oh God! Let's get down to the safe room, now!" shouted Rue as she and Colleen bolted out of the office, hand in hand, and headed to the apparent safety of the basement.

Just as they reached the basement, there was the sound of an explosion outside in the grounds, which shattered glass in the building. The two women instinctively ducked as they ran through the basement opening to safety.

In the chaos, Colleen was aware that others were right behind her, and on entering the basement saw that Rob, Shane, and Mary were already there. It seemed like a lot longer, but soon, all the occupants of the building were safe inside the bunker, including Jim, Colleen, of course, and Watson and Holmes.

Most of them were in shock and disbelief, except Ron and Jim, who had experienced similar episodes during their government and military service. They tried to reassure the distraught others that they were now safe, at least for the time being.

"I believe we have shot down a couple of drones," said Jim, looking at his phone. "Hopefully, this will be over soon."

The team had never been in this situation during their time at Bletchley, and it brought home for all of them the difference between the idea of being part of a conflict and the experience of being at war. It represented the metamorphosis of a disembodied idea into a real sensation of threat and danger that they were all now experiencing. The difference between conscious rationality and a subconscious impression now permeated their mind-bodies.

Eventually, there was nothing but silence from above. Jim answered his phone and reported the update.

"It looks like the attack has been thwarted. There's some damage to the outer buildings and the main entrance to this place, but it looks minimal. No casualties reported as of yet. We'll need to stay down here for a few minutes to ensure our safety. Security is checking the grounds, right now. No signs of any more drones."

Despite the obvious collective sigh of relief, their individual and collective experience of their work at Bletchley had been forever changed.

The group eventually made their way out of the basement and were surprised to see that apart from a few glass shards in the hallway, everything looked the same as it had before the attack.
However, as much as it might have looked the same, it didn't feel the same.

Shane suggested that the team break for the day and give themselves time to recoup and refocus.

"I'm fine with that," said Colleen, "but if Mary, Shane, or Rob want to chat, I'd be happy to talk with you."

Rob, declined, saying he wanted to ensure Noel and all the computer systems were operating normally. Shane asked to postpone until tomorrow, but Mary volunteered to talk shortly. Colleen and Mary agreed to meet in half an hour.

The group dispersed, with Colleen asking Jim, Holmes, and Watson to accompany her to the office.

"Well, that was interesting," said Holmes.

The others asked what he was referring to.

Holmes commented that he was watching the women in particular, very closely, as the attack was ongoing.

"And what did you perceive, Sherlock?" asked Jim.

"Mary seemed appropriately shaken by the ordeal. Her sparkling self seemed to go flat with anxiety. Sandra, on the other hand, didn't seem at all bothered, and in fact, looked almost bored. Rue abandoned her controlled organized self and was an emotional mess."

"What do you imply from those observations?" asked Jim.

"Well, one thing that jumped out at me was that Sandra had very little emotional reaction to a dangerous situation. That seemed abnormal, but also consistent with some suspicion we have about her that she could be devious and a downright liar. Seems a bit psychopathic to me," said Holmes.

"But perhaps the main thing was Rue. Her controlled demeanor disintegrated. It makes me concerned about her. I think now more than ever that she is hiding something, something that runs very deep. I hope that Colleen can get to the bottom of it."

"Definitely a possibility and a very good observation, Sherlock, especially when I tell you what happened just prior to the attack," said Colleen before continuing.

"I was in the middle of my interview with Rue when the alarm sounded. But just prior to that, she went blank as if she had faded away, she dissociated. We were talking about her sister's death and her ensuing depression. She went very quiet and was briefly unresponsive. And then the alarm went off and she came back quickly. I will definitely need to follow up with her."

Holmes was particularly interested in this news but kept his increased curiosity under wraps for now.

Jim then asked the psychologist of the nature of Rue's dissociative episode.

"She just went blank, as if she had faded away. She wasn't there with me for a short while. I'm not sure what would have happened if the alarm hadn't sounded. I suspect that I would have found out a lot more about her sister's tragic accident. Talking of which, do we have any details of what actually happened to her sister? I think that is going to be very relevant. Can we find out, Jim?"

Jim agreed that the information about Rue's sister's death was important for understanding Rue but was still unsure of whether it had anything to do with Nat's death. Holmes and Watson agreed with Jim's comments. He agreed to relay the need for information about Rue's sister's death to the relevant authority back at MI6. He then invited Colleen to explain in a bit more detail what dissociation involves so that Holmes and Watson could grasp the importance of her work with Rue.

"Dissociation comes when someone is traumatized. The trauma is so great and unmanageable that the person effectively removes themselves from the scene. Sometimes during the traumatic event, they lose consciousness or even have an out-of-the-body experience and might even see themselves from a different, independent perspective, like from above. The traumatic experience is then recorded in the subconscious and out of conscious awareness because the memory is too painful. It becomes separated." Colleen paused to ensure she still had the attention of Holmes and Watson.

"Sometimes an alter ego is developed automatically to deal with the trauma and memory. That alter ego is the keeper of the secret, and generally has their own perspective on the event. The goal in therapy, for example, is to access the alter ego and find out the details that have remained hidden from the person. Then you can gradually present the person with those memories, and once accessed, there's no longer a need for a secret keeper and the alter ego disappears. The alter ego is a protector that can help the person avoid revisiting the trauma, which can be both a good thing and a bad thing."

Dr. Watson commented that the subconscious was truly amazing and seriously underestimated.

"The brain has very limited storage space. It is impossible for us to remember even a small percentage of things that happen to us, but that information is stored in our mind-bodies, potentially every cell in our bodies. We have the encyclopedias of our experiences buried in the remote libraries of our cells. Those encyclopedias sometimes convey their knowledge through feelings. That is the basis of intuition."

Colleen remarked that it wasn't just personal experiences that were hidden in the subconscious, but important life lessons.

"That's why Hubert Dreyfus said robots need bodies in order to be intelligent. The body is key to our understanding life, as well as accessing experiences. I generally agree with his notion that experience comes before knowledge, not the other way round."

"Well, it will be very interesting to see what remains hidden in Rue's subconscious. Colleen, the sooner we can find out, the sooner we can determine whether this has anything to do with Nat's death," said Jim.

Colleen agreed and was determined to follow-up with Rue as soon as possible.

Watson then changed the topic.

"What's the odds of another attack, Jim?"

Jim responded that another attack was not very likely but certainly not impossible. But the attack had given MI6 and the other security services valuable information about the nature of likely attacks, the weapons used, the probable timing and directions, all of which would be valuable in early detection and effective defense.

"So, don't rule it out but don't sweat over it, either," said Jim.

"By the way, Colleen have you interviewed Sandra yet?" asked Holmes. "I think it would be good if you followed up with her.

There's something that's not right with that woman."

Colleen agreed to follow-up as soon as possible, maybe this evening.

Chapter Twenty-Three

Friday: 7:30pm

"Speech was given to man to disguise his thoughts."
Charles Maurice de Talleyrand

That evening during Sandra's break, she met with Colleen.

The women exchanged pleasantries as they sat down in Colleen's temporary office. Colleen looked around to ensure that the door was firmly shut and listened intently to ensure no-one could hear their conversation.

"Well, Sandra, my dear girl, Sherlock Holmes is on to you. He observed you being fearless during this afternoon's raid and thought that was untypical of a simple receptionist," said Colleen.

"That bloke is very smart. And, of course, he thought I was lying to him about my past when I denied any involvement with that Meth Lab deal. That's a problem. If Ron knew the truth, he certainly wouldn't have complicated things and got Holmes concerned about me," said Sandra.

Sandra continued. "I remember the discussion we had at headquarters about whether Ron should be told about my real identity. We decided against it, and I think that was the right decision, but it meant that Ron was somewhat misled about me and led down the wrong path. And then of course when we were in the basement during the raid, I forgot to act like a freaked-out receptionist."

"Well, I guess you acted like your true self. A special investigator for MI6, Karen," said Colleen before quickly correcting herself, "I mean Sandra." The two of them laughed quietly.

"Should we tell Holmes and Ron who I really am?" asked Sandra.

"You mean the woman who exposed the meth lab? The woman who uncovered the spy ring within the defense department? The woman who was especially chosen for this role so the department could keep eyes on what was going on here? I think old Sherlock might feel a bit intimidated if he were given all that information, and Ron would probably be apoplectic," said Colleen.

Karen, aka Sandra, responded. "You're right. We shouldn't tell him anything. I think that if they and the others find out that MI6 has been watching them all along, it could change the entire atmosphere and investigation. And then they might even get suspicious of us, which wouldn't be good at all. So, let's keep our damned mouths shut and let them figure it out if they have to. We don't want them thinking that the government had anything to do with this, do we?" she said rhetorically.

"Should I tell them that I know for a fact neither Shane nor Ron left their ground floor bedrooms on the night in question?"

Colleen thought about it for a while.

"Yes, I think you could. I do believe that they already think that Ron has a watertight alibi and Shane is the least likely suspect, so there'd be no harm in telling them if they ask you. Or you could just be ambivalent and not say anything. I'd like us to stay on top of things."

Chapter Twenty-Four

Saturday: 9:00am

*"Science is a way of thinking much more than it is a
body of knowledge."*
Carl Sagan

Watson decided to return to London for the weekend to catch up on some of his university chores and also attend the American football game at Tottenham Hotspur stadium on Sunday. He told Holmes he would be available to return with an hour's notice if the need should arise. Holmes was anticipating a less demanding day, with a scheduled interview with Matt, the groundskeeper, and creating more diversionary topics for Rob and Noel to investigate.

Matt was a large man with a dark flowing beard. He had only been informed about Nat's passing the day before, when he was also reminded about his oath of secrecy. Before being interviewed by Holmes he offered the detective a tour of the spectacular grounds, which Sherlock graciously accepted. Sherlock marveled at the man's knowledge and practical skills that created and maintained the beautiful landscape. The tour also gave Holmes the opportunity to ask Matt about the wildlife and particularly the rodent life.

"I think the pest control company do a pretty good job of controlling the pests. Sandra can get a little peeved if she sees one anywhere near the kitchen," volunteered Matt, "but I don't think that happens very much."

Sensing the opportunity to open up some discrete questioning, Holmes asked Matt about his impression of Sandra.

"She's pretty good at what she does. I think the others like her, or at least tolerate her. Except perhaps for Nat."

Holmes asked the groundskeeper what he meant by his comment about the relationship between Sandra and Nat.

"Well, they seemed close. I'd sometimes see Nat in the kitchen chatting with Sandra in the evening and they seemed to be enjoying each other's company. Not that I am implying anything was going on between them, but I do remember one time, they seemed to be really laughing it up together. And I hardly ever saw Nat doing that before. That's all," said Matt. "I didn't see much of Nat because he too was working with them robots."

At that point they reached the part of the property that bore the brunt of the recent drone attack. Some trees were dismembered, and a lot of greenery destroyed.

"I gotta get working on restoring this today. It's gonna take a few weeks if not longer to get this back to where it was," said Matt. "Is this going to happen again?" he asked Sherlock.

Holmes shrugged his shoulders indecisively and then asked Matt what his impression was of the other members of the team.

"The other ladies are nice and always polite to me. I don't see much of Rob because he's always down in the basement with the robots. I have a few doubts about Earl, if I'm honest. He can be a bit too fond of himself, even a bit smug, if I may say so. Not that I see him that much, but I have spotted him walking around the garden on his phone and he can get very…er…," Matt hesitated as he searched for the right word. "Very excitable. He can get very worked up." Holmes asked about Matt's impression of the other team members.

"Dr. Shane is really a great guy. A real pleasure to work for. Now, that Ron guy," again Matt hesitated searching for the accurate description for Ron. "He's okay but lately he seems to have been a lot more frustrated and quicker to blow a fuse. He hasn't always been like that, just in the last couple of months. Not quite sure why but I think it is noticeable. I'm sure you have asked the others about it. I wonder whether they sense the same thing?"

Sherlock changed the subject and asked Matt where he was on the night of the murder.

"I was at home with my wife. We were probably asleep by 10 in the evening. I'm an especially early riser and go to bed pretty early. It's really shocking what happened to Nat."

Holmes asked Matt whether he noticed anything unusual in the days just before the incident.

"No, nothing at all. I have been trying to rack my brains, but nothing is coming."

After a few more inconsequential comments, Holmes ended the interview and encouraged Matt to go and tend to the damaged landscape.

After a short break, Holmes went to visit Dr. Rob in the basement, where Noel had some new insights.

"I have some answers to those questions you asked me," said Rob as they say down opposite each other.

"The data on the relationship on belief in heaven and murder is rather inconclusive. There are some studies that actually suggest belief in heaven might make one more likely to commit crime in general and murder in particular, but others that suggest the reverse association. The studies suggest that the moral basis of religion encourages self-control, as does social participation and support," summarized Rob.

After a little thought, Holmes wondered whether murderers who believed in heaven may justify their actions on the grounds that they are sending those killed to a much better place. Dr. Rob looked cynically at Holmes, who then continued, "After all, human beings aren't rational, they're storytellers who can justify almost anything they want to."

Dr. Rob continued reviewing his notes. "Now, on the subject of left-handedness, of course some murderers are left-handed. However, some studies conducted in African and Pacific countries show there is a correlation between the number of left-handed people in the society and violent crime. One suggestion is that left-handers have an advantage in physical fights because right-handers are not trained or ready for left-handed attacks, and thus left-handedness, at least in some societies, is more likely to be inclined to violence. Because left-handedness has a genetic component the notion is that left-handers may have more violence somewhere in their genes."

"Well, the only left-handed person of interest is Earl. What do you make of that?" asked Sherlock.

"Well, that's certainly a possibility, Holmes, but I wouldn't put too much money on that bet, just yet, or at least not for that reason," said Rob.

"So that's the latest on your questions for Noel and myself. Do you have anything else?" asked Rob.

"Actually, I do. I recently saw an article that suggested the number 13 was related to crime and especially murderers. Interestingly, the notion was posed that killers are likely to have 13 letters in their names. For example, Jeffrey Dahmer was a notorious killer who had thirteen letters in his name. So did Charles Manson. I know it sounds a bit fanciful, but could you do a data search and analysis on this matter?"

Rob was more than a bit cynical -- until Sherlock spoke again.

"And, of course, one of your key suspects does indeed have thirteen letters in their name," said Holmes.

"They do?" asked Rob as he quickly considered who Holmes was referencing.

"The name Earl Bestinnie, has thirteen letters does it not?"

There was a pause, after which Holmes said, "And so does Shane Kenwight, not that he seems to be a suspect, but you would know, Rob, you never know where the data will lead you."

And with that, Sherlock thought he had lured Dr. Rob into another potentially futile search of mass data.

The conversation had returned Rob's thoughts to his likeliest perpetrators, Earl and Ron.

"Sherlock, may I ask you a question?"

"Of course," said Holmes trying to anticipate Rob's thought process.

"What, if anything, has anyone said about Ron?"

When Sherlock looked perplexed, Rob clarified his thinking.

"Well, I have noticed him get unusually angry and frustrated lately. I wonder whether anyone else has reported the same feeling?"

"Why do you ask?"

"Well, I have uncovered some research that suggests some murders are committed by people who have developed brain injuries, especially in their frontal lobe area. And often, such people were reported to have changed their character and become uncharacteristically aggressive in the time leading up to the murder. Ron worries me from that perspective. Is his recent behavior change symptomatic of such a brain injury, and does it make him a serious suspect?"

Holmes reported that he was familiar with Dr. Adrian Raine, a criminal neurologist and his work on frontal lobe injury and psychopathy.

"I do believe that Ron has a very strong alibi, but until we get to the bottom of this thing, we'll never know for sure about anyone," said Sherlock. "And that even includes Noel," he added.

"What! You think Noel is a person, I mean a computer, of interest?! Have you lost your mind, Holmes!"

"No, of course, I don't believe that Noel had anything to do with this crime. But I would be interested to know what experts like yourself see as the ways AI can be used for criminal purposes."

Rob relaxed after seeing that Holmes was not suggesting that Noel had anything to do with Nat's death and acknowledged that the relationship between AI and crime was indeed an interesting topic and one that he had been involved in researching.

Rob searched his files briefly and then found a summary of research on the dangers of Artificial Intelligence that he had scraped from various articles on the internet. He read it for Sherlock.

"The main areas where robots themselves inflict damage are military robots, drones, and driverless vehicles, where the technology is taken over and used in a harmful way. Of course, we don't know how far military applications have gone as that is top secret information.

Also, there's concern about AI taking over and disrupting infrastructure, like what happened on that CIA attack that send toxic fumes into the building. However, in the research field there's considerably more concern about larger scale crime that affects many people and even society at large. This includes such things as scams and phishing operations that extort millions of pounds from innocent people.

There is even more concern about the creation of fake news, often maximized through the use of manipulated videos, that will seriously mislead people and have a major impact on cultural tensions, politics and civic upheaval. This is where foreign enemies can not only influence elections but create massive societal division, which can seriously threaten the entire society.

So, the likeliest way that AI could lead to a death like Nat's was convincing someone through fake news, that Nat needed to be taken out. That's much more likely than a robot like Noel actually committing the murder."

Chapter Twenty-Five

Saturday: 11:30am

"Our normal waking consciousness, rational consciousness as we call it, is but one special type of consciousness, whilst all about it, parted from it by the filmiest of screens, there lie potential forms of consciousness entirely different."
William James

It was time for Rue to meet with Colleen again.

Colleen had already scripted her actions and first remarks to Rue before she invited the Chief Administrator back into her office to follow-up on their first session.

As Colleen sat down, she looked a little distracted and confused.

"I'm sorry, Rue, there's so much going on, I have lost my focus for a moment. What did we talk about last time?" she asked, knowing full well what was discussed at the previous session.

Rue sat back thoughtfully.

"We talked about the team, my relationship with them and Nat, and that sort of thing."

"I'm sorry my mind is blank at the moment. Was there anything else?" asked the psychologist.

Colleen was obviously trying to determine how much of the previous session Rue recalled, or whether she even remembered losing time.

"No, I don't think so. It was all about Nat. But then that damned alarm went off! That whole thing freaked me out," said Rue.

Colleen asked how the attack had influenced Rue.

"Initially I was freaked out, but since then I have been back to my normal self."

"What is that normal self, Rue? What's your default emotional state?" asked the psychologist.

Rue responded that she considered herself pretty strong. She expressed gratification that she had learned through adversity how to manage emotions and stay focused.

"Have you ever practiced mindfulness or meditation techniques? Those can definitely help with managing one's emotions," commented Colleen.

"I have never felt that I needed to do anything like that. I just tell myself to focus, and I almost always can," said Rue.

"What's your sleep like?"

"Generally, pretty good, but once in a while I do have a bad dream. If I wake up, sometimes it takes me a while to get back to sleep but overall, I'd say my sleep is fine. Why do you ask?"

"Well, I know that people who have suffered from depression often have sleep difficulties. Oh, that's what we were talking about last time, your depression. Do you recall us talking about that?"

Rue thought about it for a moment. "I think you asked me what medication I had been on."

"We also talked about how you coped with the death of your sister?" remarked Colleen pointedly and watched very closely to observe Rue's reaction to the introduction of this very sensitive topic.

Rue inhaled deeply at the mention of her dead sister. She fell silent.

"Can you tell me what happened to your sister?"

"No, I can't. It's the one thing that is too difficult for me to talk about," said Rue defiantly.

"Were the two of you close?"

Rue couldn't reply, but eventually nodded her head to assure the psychologist that they were indeed close. Very close.

The room was filled with silence, a noisy silence that implied that words were not welcome at this moment.

Rue suddenly reached up in a grimace and put her head in her hands.

"I have a terrible headache. Oh my God. I'm sorry but I think I need to lay down. I'm sorry but I must go back to my room. I also need to get some aspirin from Allison right away. Oh my God! I'm so sorry."

Colleen helped Rue to her feet and escorted her to find Allison, who duly provided her with a bottle of aspirin. Colleen led Rue back to her room and made sure she was safe and laying on the bed. She watched as Rue swallowed the aspirin, knowing that the aspirin wasn't going to help that much.

As Rue was stretched out on her bed, falling into a sleep, Colleen spoke softly and rhythmically to her.

"It's okay Rue. You are back in control. The pain in your head is only temporary and will recede and return now from where it came. You can relax. Calm and relaxed. Calm and in control. Relaxed and in control."

Colleen repeated these words for a few minutes, until Rue was sound asleep. At least for now.

When Colleen left Rue's room she was called by Jim who asked her to come down to his office. When she arrived she found Rob also there.

"Rob and Noel believe they have identified the perpetrator," said Jim. "Rob, please explain your findings to Colleen."

Colleen sat down and eagerly listened to what Rob had to say.

"As you know, Noel firmly believes that the murderer was a male. I know it was neither me nor Shane so that just leaves Earl and Ron. Both of them have some potentially serious mental issues," said Rob looking at Colleen for affirmation.

"Please continue," said the psychologist without offering any response to Rob's suggestion.

"There's overwhelming evidence that Ron has had some very obvious and serious mood changes in the past few weeks that Noel and I believe are indicative of some brain disorder, probably a tumor. And, as you know, Colleen, such tumors are very common in murderers.”

“Well, certainly some serial killers but I’m not sure what percentage of murders such a problem actually accounts for,” replied Colleen.

“Nonetheless, Noel and I are convinced and have a mass of data on our side that the killer is a man and we believe that for the reasons I have just outlined, Ron is the murderer.”

“Thank you for sharing your opinion with us, Rob. However, we still need to continue with our own investigations before we can definitively conclude that Ron is the murderer. In the meantime, please say nothing to anyone at all – no-one – about this until we are able to confirm your suspicions,” said Jim.

Chapter Twenty-Six

Sunday: 8:00am

"Disinformation is more than just lying: it's the denial and twisting of reality in order to present some desired image to the rest of the world."
Will Hurd

Sherlock was taking an early morning walk around the splendid grounds of the Range when his phone rang. It was Ron. He told Holmes that there had been a major development and that everyone was called to the conference room.

When Sherlock arrived, everyone else was there and Ron had a screen up, as if he were about to give a presentation. On closer inspection, Holmes saw the screen was showing the front page of *The Sunday Times* newspaper. Then he saw the headline.

"Chinese Claim Murder of Leading AI Expert."

The story reported a press release from the Chinese government which announced the death of Nat Gurnal, a leading British AI expert working against them in Bletchley in the United Kingdom.

The release claimed that Chinese agents had managed to penetrate security and kill the famed AI expert, although details weren't provided on exactly how Nat was killed.

Jim invited the group's thoughts on the release. There was general unease and a decent amount of skepticism amongst the group.

"If they had really done this, they would have announced it a lot sooner," said Holmes. "I am guessing they have just hacked someone or something, and only now found out about Nat's murder and are trying to capitalize on it. There would be no reason to wait, if they knew and if they did it, they would have known almost a week ago."

Jim agreed and pointed out that there was a photoshopped picture in the release that was meant to be Nat's bedroom, but closer examination showed that it was not his room.

"This tells us merely that someone has been hacked and the news about Nat's death is now public knowledge," said Ron.

"That could be literally anyone working at MI6, or the organization itself, or any one of us, or people working under us, or our own infrastructure. Let's get on this right away and see if we are the ones, individually or organizationally, who have been hacked," said Ron.

As usual Earl was a bit skeptical of the narrative that was being created.

"Are we really sure that someone like Khang isn't responsible for the murder and/or the leak?"

"Well, even if he was, why would the Chinese wait to put out the release? It's not like they had to wait until Khang was safely out of the country, or anything like that," said Ron, to the general agreement of the others.

Sherlock then commented that it was only yesterday when Dr. Rob was explaining the possible misuses of AI and claimed that this sort of fake news was considered amongst the most dangerous developments in artificial intelligence.

Mary then asked Jim what the official response to the Chinese claim would be.

"I have been in touch with Lori, the Chief Press Officer and she told me that the government is preparing a statement that denies the Chinese propaganda and will report that Nat had indeed died, but of natural causes," said Jim.

"Will there be any mention of us?" asked Rue.

"No, I don't believe so, although of course the Chinese know exactly where we are," said Jim.

"In some ways, I think this indicates the challenges facing the Chinese right now. They will be looking for any ways to distract and deny the serious challenges they are confronting right now on the front lines and at home. This sort of fake news is just what they were looking for," said Ron. "Let's not have it influence our perceptions of reality."

The group agreed that they remain super vigilant to the possibility of another physical drone attack and work together to investigate the possibility of a cyber-attack. They then spent the rest of the morning checking both personal and organizational systems to ensure they were secure and, in the process, found nothing significant. Their cyber-defenses were still working well.

By the time most of the group congregated for a late lunch, there was another development that would have a significant impact on their operations.

Chapter Twenty-Seven

Sunday: 1:00pm

"Occurrences in this domain are beyond the reach of exact prediction because of the variety of factors in operation, not because of any lack of order in nature."
Albert Einstein

Most of the group had reconvened for lunch and were enjoying their desserts when Ron got a text message.

It was from Grant Renier, the CEO of IntualityAI, the predictive analytics company.

Call me asap. I may have something for you.

Ron told Jim and Colleen about the text, and they headed out to Ron's office as he texted Renier back with details to access their cyber protected video conference system immediately.

As the trio sat around Ron's desk, Grant appeared on the large monitor. It was still early morning in North Carolina.

Renier greeted the group and immediately referenced the latest Chinese news release about their killing Nat.

"Is there any truth to that?" he asked.

"No, just a lot of propaganda. They need something to lift their spirits at the moment," said Jim.

Grant knew that further questions or even debate about the issue of Nat's death was a waste of time because of security protocol, so he got straight to the point.

"As you know we have been tracking the Chinese economy for months now, and this morning, Intuality produced an actionable alert."

The Bletchley group listened patiently.

"Basically, Intuality is predicting there will be a major downturn in the Chinese economy this week," reported Renier.

"When will this occur exactly?" asked Ron.

"Can't be too sure, but I would predict Wednesday at the latest, possibly as soon as late Monday," the predictions expert replied.

"How severe will this downturn be?" Jim asked.

"Pretty severe. It will likely affect every sector, including currency. Not quite a crash but petty close," said Renier.

The group wanted to know how confident Renier was in the prediction.

"Well, you can never be certain, but the system is pretty confident."

Renier showed them "the cube," a graphic representation of probabilities that illustrated a high wave, signaling a lot of confidence in the alert.

After further discussion in which Renier showed, explained, and shared the data, the call was ended.

Ron and Jim were particularly enthused by this news and were already considering how the government could utilize the prediction. They both seemed to think that it could be the perfect rejoinder to the fake Chinese news about Nat's death, moreover one that would confine that story to the back pages or even the scrap heap.

When the relevant departmental and government sources received the prediction, they had to decide whether to go with it or simply ignore it. A great prediction, especially the immediate performance of a financial market, is right about 60 percent of the time. However, if it were right, the opportunities to inflict serious damage on China and its war effort were enormous.

Eventually, the government authorities decided to trust the prediction. They agreed to immediately publicize the imminent decline in the Chinese economy, which in itself would likely spook investors and contribute to the loss of confidence in the Chinese market. And they decided something else. Now was the right time to up the pressure on the Chinese in every sphere: Militarily, diplomatically, economically, publicly, and in every other way possible.

While the various government and allied agencies were coordinating their latest, multivariate assaults, Watson arrived back at Bletchley.

"How was the game?" asked Sherlock as he opened the door and welcomed his friend back to the Range, referencing the American Football game at Tottenham Hotspur stadium.

"Very good, thank you," said Watson. "I followed Intuality's most confident predictions, and I won a decent amount of money. The game was interesting, too. Went down to the wire. It was a fun afternoon." Watson then asked his colleague what had happened while he was gone.

"Not too much," said Holmes before adding, "Noel hasn't found anything conclusive on the thirteen-letter name theory, yet."

"Well, what a surprise," said Watson sardonically, before heading to his room.

Chapter Twenty-Eight

Monday: 10:00am

"There is no birth of consciousness without pain."
Carl Jung

It was Rue's birthday, not that she or anyone else at the Range felt like celebrating. She was turning forty-nine today, but she didn't really care. Sandra had made a special cake for her that was eaten at breakfast and presented the opportunity for the team to wish her well, but that was it. She made her way to Colleen's office and gracefully welcomed her.

"I'm so sorry about what happened a couple of days ago," Rue said sincerely.

She told the psychologist that she had slept well but was still feeling occasionally a "a bit foggy." At least that horrendous headache had gone away.

In response to Colleen's question, Rue couldn't identify too many times when she had a headache that bad.

"I'd like to use a relaxation technique with you, today. Would that be okay?" asked the psychologist.

Rue nodded in the affirmative.

"As long as I don't get another headache," she said.

Before long, Rue was stretched out on the couch in the psychologist's office, seemingly very relaxed.

"Rue, I'd like you to imagine that you are walking down a long pathway towards a large house."

After a few seconds, Colleen inquired whether Rue could see herself doing that.

Rue vocalized a very soft affirmation.

"Now, Rue, you are entering the house. You are in a large foyer. There is a steep stairway to your right."

Rue again confirmed she was there and could see the stairway.

"Now turn to your left, and you will see a white door."

Rue confirmed she was there.

"Now open the door and you will see some stairs that lead down to the lower level."

"When you reach this lower level, you can see a hallway. It's just like a hotel corridor with numbered rooms on each side of the carpeted floor."

Colleen waited briefly for Rue's acknowledgement before continuing.

"Turn to the first door on your right. It's number 49."

"Now, walk slowly down the corridor. As you walk slowly, you pass the rooms on your right.
47…45…43…41…39…37…35…33…31…29…27…25… 23…
Stop there and open the door to room number 23. What do you see?"

After a short pause Rue spoke.

"I see some of my friends from college. We are studying together for an exam. It looks like we are in the university library."

"Which part of the library are you in?"

"The study section to the right of where all the books are," said Rue quietly.

"Can you identify your friends?"

"There's Allie, Susie, Laurie, and one more…oh, that's Kirsten," said Rue.

"It looks like we are the only ones there. I can see shelves of books off to the left."

"Very good," said the psychologist. "Do you see anything else?"

Rue indicated she couldn't see anything else.

Colleen suggested that Rue leave this room, cross over the hallway, and enter room number 18.

"Let me know when you're there," Colleen said, and before long Rue signaled that she was by the door of room number 18. The psychologist suggested she enter the room.

Colleen saw Rue smile as she recalled a memory from her school days, and then prompted her recall more.

"We are in the school canteen having lunch," said Rue. "There's Velinda, Heather, Megan, Kelly, Stephanie and, let's see," said Rue as she was clearly trying to identify some of the others.

"Then there's Tara, Cindy, Doreen, Nancy, Monique, Elaine, Lauren, and Joy," Rue said slowly as she was able to recall the names of the people that her visual memory was presenting to her.

"Oh, and the girls with their cute hats. What were their names?" Rue paused for a moment. "Ah yes, Kris, Janet and Linda."

"Ok," said Colleen. "Now leave the room, close the door and keep heading down the hallway. You are passing the rooms on the right….17…15…13…11…9…7. Open the door to room number seven. What do you see?"

After a short pause Rue said, "I see my friend Molly. We are playing with her dog, Shadow. There's someone else there but I can't make out who it is."

Colleen again encouraged Rue to look for more details.

"We are in Molly's back yard. It's a sunny day. Shadow is chasing a ball that Molly has thrown."

Colleen then said, "Rue, you can leave this room now. See yourself exiting the room and closing the door. Now leave this room and turn left to head back up the corridor. That's number nine and now eleven. Now you are by room eleven. Open the door and enter room eleven."

There was a short silence. Then Rue spoke with more than a little anxiety in her voice.

"I can't open the door. It's locked."

"No, it's not locked. It's open. You just need to push a little harder and the door will open," said Colleen.

"I can't' get it open. It's stuck," said Rue anxiously.

"One more push and it will open, I promise you," said the psychologist.

"Oh, yes it has opened. But...but...there's nothing here," said Rue stressfully.

"Try to look harder and you'll see it."

"No, I can't see anything here. There's a thick fog or something, in this place. I need to get out of here!" Rue said in a panicked voice. "Please let me out of here!"

Colleen observed Rue falling into some kind of stupor. Her expression became blank, her eyes seemed lifeless.

The psychologist waited.

Suddenly, Rue became aroused. Her expression changed, and she lifted her head slowly, looking Colleen directly into her eyes.

Then her lips moved, and a voice emanated from within her.

"I am a doctor, and I would ask that you please do not put us through this again," said a male voice.

"Who are you?" asked the psychologist.

"I am a doctor. It was very messy and difficult."

"What was messy and difficult?" asked Colleen trying to stay calm.

"You know what I am talking about," said Rue's male alter ego before adding, "I have to leave, I have a terrible headache coming on."

At which point Rue became silent once more and slumped back onto the couch.

"Rue can you hear me?" asked Colleen.

Rue grunted softly.

Colleen continued in the hope that she still had access to Rue.

"Okay, Rue, you can leave the room now. Just step outside and close the door. Now turn left and head back down the corridor to the door at the end of the hallway."

Rue again grunted softly, which Colleen took as a sign of her following instructions.

"Raise your hand when you reach the door at the end of the hallway," said Colleen.

Within a few short seconds, Rue raised her hand gently.

"Okay, now open the door and climb up the stairs back to the lobby."

Once again, Rue raised her hand when asked to do so when she was in the lobby.

"Okay, good. Now exit out of the front door of the building and head down the driveway."

Several minutes later, Rue opened her eyes.

"Wow, how long have I been asleep?" she asked while checking her watch. "I feel a bit headachy again," she said frowning.

"What do you remember?" asked Colleen.

"I remember just laying down on this couch. Don't remember anything after that, until now. What happened?"

The psychologist reassured Rue that nothing had happened and that she had just been in a hypnotic state for about twenty minutes.

"Rue, we need to continue with these sessions. I think you'll eventually find them very helpful."

"Did I say anything in the hypnosis? I don't remember anything at all."

The psychologist commented that it was unclear what Rue had said, which is why she wanted to continue doing the hypnosis. They arranged to meet early the next day.

Chapter Twenty-Nine

Tuesday: 9:00am

"Whatever we plant in our subconscious mind and nourish with repetition and emotion will one day become a reality."
Earl Nightingale

It had now been over a week since Nat's murder. Theories and suspicions ran wild, but it wasn't obvious which of them had the most, or any, validity. But Noel and Rob believed that it was now obvious that Ron was the likeliest suspect.

It was time for Rue to have another session with Colleen. She admitted to Colleen that she was very apprehensive about the upcoming session but intuitively felt that it was necessary. Colleen found this encouraging and prepared herself for what was to come.

Rue lay down on the couch and closed her eyes, as Colleen softly and rhythmically led her into a hypnotic state. She then guided her visually down the pathway to the house that she had used in their last session. As Colleen guided Rue down through the white door and to the corridor below, she once again asked her to walk down the corridor. "49…47…45…," she repeated the decreasing numbers until Rue was at door number eleven. The room which Rue could barely access during the previous session and the room that was concealed in a traumatic fog.

"Now open the door to room number eleven," suggested Colleen.

This time, there was no resistance. The door opened and Rue stepped inside.

Colleen observed that Rue became almost lifeless and silent. She waited patiently.

"I asked you not to come here again," said a male voice, which Colleen assumed was the doctor.

"I know it's very important that I speak with you. Please allow me that," Colleen asked firmly.

"What do you want to know?" said the male voice emanating from Rue.

Colleen had seen a couple of alter egos in her career, but this was the most bizarre experience. Watching the divided Rue speak in a male voice was almost supernatural. It was like an AI meme, something from a science fiction futuristic fantasy.

"What happened?" asked Colleen in a heightened state of anticipation.

"Before I tell you, you must agree never to let anyone know what I am about to tell you."

Colleen agreed knowing that her consent was neither legally binding nor morally acceptable.

"It was a warm summer's day and Rue and her sister had decided to take a ride into the countryside," started the doctor. "Her sister had recently got her driver's license and wanted to take Rue on a fun outing. They drove to Hertfordshire and stopped in a lovely rural part of the county. They were walking along a country path admiring the scenery when suddenly, out of nowhere, came two scruffy blokes, about twenty years old. They must have been following the girls for a while. They attacked the girls and dragged them into their van which was parked nearby. They drove for a few minutes then stopped by a barn."

There was a pause before the doctor continued.

"It was there that the girls were brutally raped," said the doctor in a monotone voice.

"It was very traumatic. Rue's sister was in horrendous distress and kept calling out "Let me Die! Let me Die!" as her attacker continually forced himself on her. Rue could hear her screams, but of course, she couldn't do anything about it as she was tied up while being sexually abused herself. Part of her wanted to die, too.
May be that would have been for the best."

"Why do you say, that?" asked Colleen.

"Sometimes, people need to be put out of their misery," said the doctor.

"What happened next?" asked Colleen, shocked by the revelation.

"The two bastards left them in the barn and fled. The girls were, of course, seriously traumatized, but at least they had each other. They decided to keep the whole disgusting affair a secret, at least for the time being. They figured that they had each other and that they would try to put the experience behind them. And then, her sister died four days later."

"How did her sister die?" asked Colleen.

"She fell off a balcony."

"Look, I've never told this to anyone else. It must be kept a secret," said the doctor.

"No-one knows that this has happened?" asked the psychologist.

"Nobody, nor must they ever know. It would devastate Rue."

Colleen knew that, on the contrary, Rue must be told if she were ever to escape the horrific trauma. If Rue never found out, the trauma would stamp itself on her very soul as well as her mind and body for the rest of her life.

"What about their parents? Didn't they suspect something was wrong? How did they react when the girls came home?"

"Well," said the alter ego, "That's the point. The parents were away on vacation and didn't return until almost three days later. It was the next day that her sister died, and that occupied their entire attention. They didn't have a clue about what happened."

The psychologist thought that what she had been told was accurate, but reminded herself that this was Rue's subconscious narrative, and that it was subjective and possibly incorrect in some respects. However, Colleen knew that the trauma inflicted on Rue was great, otherwise she wouldn't need an alter ego to take responsibility for the memory and the experience.

"Were the men who did this horrendous thing ever caught?" asked Colleen.

"I don't believe so. If they were, I don't know about it. Neither of the girls knew these blokes, and of course, the crime was never reported. That's all I have."

"Well, if I need to talk to you again, I'll just ask for the doctor," said Colleen, sensing that the male alter ego was about to retire to the lower depths of the iceberg.

What she had been told made sense to Colleen. She knew it was common for the victims of such crimes to feel tremendous guilt and shame for what had happened, despite the fact that they were in no way responsible for the actions of their satanic attackers. Sometimes, that shame and guilt was planted in their brains by the perpetrators, who try to make the victims feel responsible. And the whole experience eats away at a person's confidence, feelings of safety, and their self-worth, leaving them carrying the enormous, unbearable weight of the experience.

At that point, Colleen was amazed at the mind, that it could indeed hide the horrendous experiences deep below the surface of daily existence, at the very bottom of the iceberg. She was amazed at how successful Rue had been, given the circumstances and the trauma she endured. However, the psychologist knew that some traumatized people do become very focused in an effort to fill their time with tasks and thus not be drawn into deep thought, which could go too deep, into the indescribable, into hell.

When Colleen turned back to look at Rue, she sensed that the alter ego doctor had already left, retreating into the dark gravitation cavities of the subconscious. This was a good thing, as the longer the doctor hung around the more distressed Rue would be. At the very least she would have a horrible headache – or worse.

Eventually, Rue woke up out of her hypnotized nightmare. She looked very spaced out and felt even more scattered.

As she slowly regained full consciousness, Rue asked what happened.

"Something feels different," she said, looking around the room in a panic, expecting to find clues for her disrupted self.

"What happened? What did I say?" demanded Rue. "I can definitely feel that something is different. Something's not right. My intuition is usually very accurate. What happened?" she screamed.

"You told me a little bit about your sister's passing," said Colleen, testing to see how much of what she had been told by her alter ego doctor was now consciously available to Rue.

"I did? What did I say? I don't remember mentioning any of that," said Rue.

"You told me how she died," said Colleen.

Rue instantly crumbled into a tearful, sad, helpless persona.

"I can't do this!" Rue screamed.

The psychologist was not to be distracted.

"You told me she fell off a balcony."

Rue cried even harder. Then she collected the pillow on the back of the couch and started hammering it against the back of the furniture, in a frenzied, manic fit of anger.

Colleen didn't interfere, knowing that Rue had to expel some of the built-up emotion. In fact, the psychologist appreciated that Rue was venting her feelings, that this signaled a breakdown in her characteristic lifetime defense. The wall of secrets and denial had been breached.

Colleen watched silently as Rue hammered the pillow against the couch for a good six minutes. Finally, Rue collapsed on the couch and threw the pillow to the floor.

The door had been opened, but Colleen wasn't sure how far the truth had been revealed.

"So, what happened to your sister?" the psychologist asked.

There was a long pause as Rue stared motionless into the past.

"I personally believe that she jumped off that balcony," said Rue in a forlorn voice, before crumpling again into a tearful, tragic posture.

"Why would she do that?" asked Colleen testing the limits of Rue's conscious revelations.

"I honestly don't know," said Rue. "I honestly don't know. I just don't know."

Colleen assumed from this revelation that Rue now had some conscious awareness about her sister's death but was still blocking the horrendous memories that explain why her sister would commit suicide.

Eventually, Rue came back into consciousness and into the present.

Colleen asked her a question.

"I think this is very difficult for you, but it is also crucial. How would you feel if I recommend to Dr. Kenwight that you take some time off? I'd like to get to the bottom of this. What we have started here is very important for you, and I would like to ensure it progresses. What do you think?"

Rue replied that she wasn't sure she needed a lot of time off and frankly admitted that work helped her stay focused. But she welcomed at least a reduction in duties and an immediate rest seemed like a good idea.

"However," Rue said "You're here to find the answer to Nat's death. I am concerned that you think that I have some part in it. If I have nothing to do with Nat's death, why wouldn't you refer me to a different practitioner?"

Colleen replied. "We have started this complex process and referring you to someone else to start all over again wouldn't be right. And in any event, it would have to be a practitioner sanctioned by MI6 so there's a decent chance, I would be assigned to help you anyway."

Rue nodded her head unconvincingly while starting to wonder what Colleen really knew and if she could have unknowingly had a part in Nat's demise.

Chapter Thirty

Wednesday: 2:00pm

***"I think your subconscious knows far more than your
conscious, so I trust it."***
Cornelia Parker

Rue entered Colleen's office holding her head.

"I'm so sorry. I have another one of those headaches again. But I'm willing to continue if you think it's okay," said Rue.

The psychologist knew it was more than okay. Rue's headache meant that the doctor was hovering near to consciousness and would thus be easily accessible. She acknowledged that all would be manageable and that she would ensure she protected Rue. With that assurance, Rue lay down on the couch and prepared herself for what was to come, if she could.

Colleen spent a few minutes repeating rhythmically relaxing suggestions to Rue, which made her detach from consciousness and fall into a deep hypnotic state.

"I need to speak to the doctor," said Colleen.

He quickly appeared. "I knew you would be back. What is you want to know this time?" he asked.

"What happened on Sunday evening?" the psychologist asked.

There was a long silence, but eventually the doctor spoke.

"I believe that Nat called Rue at about midnight. Apparently he sounded very distressed and asked her to come up to his room but to be sure to do so quietly so no-one else would know that he had called and where she was going.

"We left the room and headed across to Nat's room. We silently opened the door and saw Nat sitting on his bed crying.

"She approached him and asked him why he was so upset."

"At least I think that was the sequence of events. At this point I became much more aware of what was going on. He told me that he could no longer live with himself. The thought of being responsible for thousands of deaths was simply unbearable for him. He could never live with himself for what he had done. He just couldn't accept that his actions, brilliant and patriotic actions, had killed several thousand young men and women. It was simply too much for him to bear."

"I tried to reassure him that his was a noble effort and in a war, which the enemy had started, people had to die. He was a hero, not a murderer. But he couldn't or wouldn't hear me. He denied he was a hero. He kept calling himself a cold-blooded murderer and no longer wanted to live. That's when he told me that he had poisoned himself. He had taken some poison that he had found on the property which apparently the exterminators had left. But it wasn't working. At least not yet. He pleaded with me to kill him by whatever means we wished. And that's when it happened."

"What happened?" asked the psychologist.

"He said softly and desperately into my ears, 'Let me die. Please let me die!'"

Thoughts flooded through Rue of that unimaginable moment when she and her sister were being traumatized. Of Rue being tied up and brutally raped while hearing her sister calling out in desperation and in search of the end. And then memories of her sister's suicide flooded horrifically into view. It was too much. That's when I took full control of the situation.

"As Nat lay down on his bed in acute distress, I picked up a pillow and suffocated him. He needed to be put out of his misery. He resisted a little at first and then surrendered peacefully. He was finally at peace, a place where he would never be if he remained on this earth. I knew it was what he wanted and what he needed. I am a doctor and know what people need."

"I left Nat's room. I quietly closed the door and returned to my room. Rue was out of it at this point and fell asleep right away. She woke up a couple of hours later with some awful sense that something was horribly wrong. She assumed she had a nightmare but didn't realize what a nightmare it really was. She fell back asleep and awoke in the morning with absolutely no memory of what had happened. Another secret for me to keep."

"I don't regret doing it. I regret that I had to do it. Another trauma for me to keep in the black hole of the subconscious. Another trauma for me to hide. Another trauma that must be kept away from Rue. It's not her fault. She has had to bear the unbearable, imagine the unimaginable. She can't do it. Who could?"

Colleen thanked the alter ego for the truth – the unbearable truth. But the truth has to be known otherwise we descend into a world of fantasy and make believe. Running from the truth only leads you down the path to hell. Colleen now knew the truth and she had a major problem as a result. She had to tell Rue her appalling reality. When she did, the doctor would no longer be needed and disappear.

There would be no more haunting, horrific secrets, or alter egos to guard them and keep them safe and concealed. But could Rue survive the truth? Only time would tell.

Eventually, the doctor disappeared, and Rue fell back into the welcoming arms of sleep. At the time, she had no idea that her life was forever changed.

When she awoke, Colleen suggested that she have something that would help her continue to sleep for the next few hours and duly gave her a sleeping medication, before guiding her back to her room.

When Colleen returned to her office, she called Shane, Ron, Jim, Holmes, and Watson to meet her immediately. The crime had been solved.

Before long, all those she had called assembled in her office.

There was an air of expectation, victory, and closure, but also chaos as they all clamored to know what had happened.

"It's complicated, but Rue killed Nat, sort of," announced Colleen. Her qualification led to puzzled looks and questions.

"What do you mean, sort of?" asked Shane.
"Please sit down and I'll explain."

"What about Rue? Shouldn't we arrest her now?" asked Ron.

Colleen assured Ron and the others that Rue was sleeping in her room and would be out for a few hours, which was plenty of time to figure out how to handle the challenges that lie ahead.

"Holmes your intuition about Rue was spot on," started Colleen. "She experienced multiple traumas in her youth that led her to develop a male alter ego to protect her from the absolute horrors of her experience," said Colleen.

"What sort of horrors?" asked Jim.

Colleen then described the rape of Rue and her sister, and her sister's plea to die. She then described how her sister had likely killed herself a few days later.

At this point Jim interjected and told the group that he had followed up Colleen's request for details about Rue sister's death and was told it was an accident, and that she fell off a balcony.

Colleen acknowledged Jim's information but expressed her opinion that she deliberately fell or jumped and killed herself.

"Oh my God!" said Holmes. "I thought she might be hiding some difficult things but nothing like this."

"Well, your intuition was right, Sherlock," said the psychologist.

"Please continue, Colleen," said Rob anxiously, wanting to know what led to Nat's death.

"The other night, Nat called Rue around midnight and asked her to come to his room. She went and when she got there, she found Nat, somewhat drowsy, sitting on his bed crying. He told her that he had tried to kill himself with poison that apparently was left by the exterminators, but that it wasn't working as quickly as he had hoped. He asked her to put him out of his misery. When she asked why he was so sad he told her that he could no longer live with himself after finding out that he was responsible for the deaths of more than three thousand young people.”

Colleen paused to keep her emotions in check.

“This interaction caused Rue to revisit her sister’s suicidal ideas and all that entailed and at that point, if not before, she completely dissociated. And that’s when her male alter ego took over, if not before.”

“Who was this male alter ego?” asked Watson.

“When people develop alter egos, they are typically versions of real or imagined characters that the person knows that fit the role of capable secret keepers and more importantly can cope with, and rationalize, the traumatic secrets they are keeping. In Rue’s case, this alter ego was a rather detached doctor figure who theoretically had the skill, experience, and persona to deal with the traumas he was now responsible for keeping. I suspect that this alter ego was a caricature of somebody she actually knew. Perhaps it was one of her father’s colleagues.”

“Nat was distressed and pleaded with Rue to let him die. Coincidentally this was also the plea that her sister made when she was being raped. The doctor may have rationalized that it would have indeed been best if her sister had died then because she killed herself a few days later anyway. And so, when Nat asked again for his life to be ended, the doctor picked up the pillow and suffocated Nat. He justified that Nat would live in trauma and in hell for the rest of his life, so he put him out of his misery.”

The group were stunned into a traumatic silence.

“You were right, Holmes, the killer was a woman,” said Watson.

"Well, not really, he was also a man," said Sherlock solemnly. "Intuality got it right. Half man, half woman, sort of."

"Where does this leave us legally?" Shane asked Jim.

"I have the entire session recorded," interjected Colleen. "There can't be much legal doubt that Rue did not know what she was doing."

"It's also possible that Nat might have died from the poison he took. It just took longer than he expected. Perhaps it was effectively a suicide. The poison would have made it difficult for Nat to resist, and certainly made his heart and breathing much more vulnerable to injury, like suffocation," said Watson.

"Good point, Watson," said Ron.

"Also," Colleen continued, "It is important to distinguish a dissociative state from a psychotic one, although they can both lead to a person being effectively and legally insane. With schizophrenia, the person is receiving thoughts and messages from outside of themselves and can believe they are being directed by some outside force to act in some way. For example, a schizophrenic might imagine that the lampshade is telling them to do something, like shoot or kill someone. Dissociation is not psychotic in that sense. Instead, the person is hijacked by an alter ego who takes over, and the person is completely unaware of what is happening. The word schizophrenia actually means 'broken soul' but that may be a more accurate description of dissociative disorder rather than psychosis."

The team unanimously agreed that Colleen's recorded evidence would prove that Rue was not in control of her behavior at the time of the murder, and that she would thus not be found guilty of homicide. She was not conscious of what she was doing, nor was she motivated to do the action.

Given his expertise in these matters, Sherlock was asked to clarify the legal situation.

"A successful Insanity defense requires the person to be unaware of their actions at the time of the crime. The actual basis of this rule is that, 'at the time of committing the act, the accused was laboring under such a defect of reason, from disease of the mind, as not to know the nature and quality of the act he was doing or, if he did know it, that he did not know what he was doing was wrong." This is called the M'Naughten Rule, and is the basis of insanity rulings in both the UK and the United States. It is named after Englishman Daniel M'Naghten, who in 1843 shot and killed the secretary of the British Prime Minister, believing that the Prime Minister was conspiring against him. I am sure that Rue would be protected under this rule."

Holmes stopped to consider possible legal options for Rue. He shared with Watson the attorneys they knew who had relevant experience in cases like this, where an insanity plea was the key to the case.

"The lawyers we know with this sort of expertise, Watson? I am thinking of Dudley, Lauren and Tim."

Watson agreed before adding, "Don't forget Jose, or Mike."

Holmes then speculated about Rue.

"She might lose her job and possibly have to serve some sort of punishment. However, she is also a very valuable member of the team, and it does seem to me that the cause of Nat's death could easily, and more correctly, be justified as a suicide. A lot will depend on Rue's subsequent mental state," he said, looking at Colleen to offer some guidance.

"Well, I don't know how Rue will be when she actually comes to face the awful truth about her past, and of course, Nat's murder. It will take some time for her to deal with it all," said Colleen.

Jim asked her whether she felt she could help Rue process these events, and if so, how long would it take. Colleen commented that it was difficult to know.

"Normally one might take weeks or even months to get from where we are now to complete processing of traumas and the revelation of hidden memories. But obviously we don't have that time. I will push it as much as I reasonably can, and let's see where we get to in a matter of days. It will be brutal for her to remember everything, but it will be much better for her in the long run, and probably even the short run. I'll schedule some long sessions with her. However, I do think we should make some contingency plans in case she completely breaks down and needs hospitalizing. In fact, as I am speaking about it, the more I see that is likely to be necessary."

Jim acknowledged the problem and told the group that he would prepare a specific London hospital for that eventuality, without naming it but implying it was a place where government agencies sent people who needed appropriate care, protection, and privacy.

Colleen approved of the idea out of necessity, but was concerned this would isolate her, too.

"One alternative would be to have a trained caregiving nurse, or even two, be here with Colleen around the clock. Keep an eye on her, prevent from doing something ill-advised, like trying to kill herself. It would be more convenient and better for her perhaps to keep her in this environment," said the psychologist.

The team decided to arrange for both contingencies and take Colleen's advice about how to move forward once she had resumed her therapy with Rue. Ron offered to contact the relevant authorities and line up two nurses who could provide twenty-four hour care if it was needed.

In the meantime, they agreed that the official conclusion was that Nat had committed suicide.

Chapter Thirty-One

Thursday: 1:00pm

"The paradox of trauma is that it has both the power to destroy and the power to transform and resurrect."
Peter A. Levine

Colleen had blocked the entire afternoon to spend with Rue. It was going to be challenging and difficult, but necessary. Rue was mildly sedated in an attempt to control her emotional response to what she was about to find out about her life and herself.

Rue relaxed on the couch in Colleen's office, not having much, or any, idea about what she was about to discover.

Colleen decided that initially at least, she would not use any specific techniques like hypnosis or EMDR – Eye Movement Desensitization and Reprocessing therapy, which was created by Dr. Francine Shapiro in 1989. The technique involves trying to reprocess traumatic memories through different sense impressions often created by tapping both sides of the body. Instead, Colleen would use whatever technique she thought would be most helpful at the moment of recall.

The key for Colleen was to identify the least challenging parts of the traumatic onion and peal them back until she eventually got to the deepest and most troubling levels – Rue and her sister being raped.

When it seemed that Rue was in the right state of consciousness, Colleen heaved a deep sigh and started the recording of the session. The goal was to get Rue's brain to recall difficult events in her life with the appropriate emotion.

"Rue, I want you to imagine yourself going into King's College hospital to visit your mother. See the entrance to the hospital and take the elevator to the third floor and the intensive care unit."

Colleen waited a few seconds.

"Go into the ward where your mother is laying in her bed. She is connected to a blood pressure monitor as well as another tube going into her other arm. Your father is sitting by her bedside holding her hand."

"Your mother is motionless and barely breathing."

Rue started to tear up. Colleen asked her to tap her forehead slowly and rhythmically. Rue followed the instruction.

"What do you see, Rue?"

Slowly Rue spoke.

"My father looks at me sadly. Then he says, 'your mother's time has come.'"

Rue broke out into a flow of soft tears. Colleen waited.

Eventually Colleen asked, "What do you see next?"

"I am holding my mother's hand. It's cold. She has passed."

"The doctor and nurses express their condolences and ask my father about the funeral arrangements," Rue added.

Then Rue burst into tears. Colleen waited for a few moments, and then encouraged Rue to relax, almost whispering rhythmic phrases to remove her from this state of sadness.

Rue had passed the first test. She could recall, with appropriate emotion, a difficult event, the passing of her mother.

After a period of calm relaxation, Colleen continued her examination of Rue's psyche.

"It's ten years ago. February 10. You get a phone call. Can you remember that?" asked Colleen.

Rue's expression changed once again. She closed her eyes.

After what seemed like several minutes Rue finally spoke.

"It's the police. They are telling me that there's been an accident. That my husband, Peter, has crashed his bike and been run over by a van. He is in the hospital in serious condition."

"What happened next?" Collen asked.

"I am stunned and panicked at the same time. But I need to get to Peter as soon as possible. I rush to get my things and head to the hospital."

"I'm driving fast and dangerously to the hospital. I narrowly miss a bus at a traffic light and freak out. Oh my God!"
Another silent pause.

"I get to the hospital and rush up to the ICU where Peter is. Where Peter was. He had died ten minutes earlier," Rue added.

Colleen waited, hoping for Rue's tears. She knew that traumatic memories were sometimes recalled without the emotion. Such numbness is part of the subconscious defense that extracts the painful emotion from the memory, presenting it as a scene devoid of any feeling.

The tears weren't forthcoming as Rue looked blankly at the wall in front of her.

Colleen probed how close to the emotions Rue was.

"Rue, you're by Peter's side. He is lifeless. You must have been distraught at his untimely death."

Rue remained emotionless; a blank expression apparently directed at Colleen but really nowhere in particular.

"How long did you stay with him?" asked Colleen trying to jumpstart Rue's consciousness.

Then it happened. Rue burst into tears. A loud, dramatic, outburst of grief.

Colleen silently felt a sense of relief. Rue was indeed able to face the traumatic horror of this significant event. She held her head in her hands and sobbed loudly.

"Two down, two to go," Colleen thought to herself. Rue had been able to access two tragic traumas, her mother's and husband's deaths. The question was whether she would be able to do the same with two more, significantly traumatic experiences, her sister's death and the horrific rape.

Colleen encouraged Rue to relax and fall asleep, as she prepared for the next critical phase of the exploration of Rue's consciousness.

As Rue slept, Colleen called Jim.

"How's it going?" Jim asked.

"So far, so good," replied Colleen. "So, I am thinking that she would probably do best with the round-the-clock nursing care, right here. You have lined some appropriate nurses up, correct?"

Jim replied that he had found two appropriate nurses, Jennifer and Julie. He would now reach out to them and arrange for one of them to be prepared to stay the night.

"When do you think we'll need her?" asked Jim.

"Late this afternoon will work," said the psychologist.

"Great," said Jim. "Good luck with the rest of the session."

While Rue slept, Colleen grabbed a snack and a drink, and checked her phone to ensure the session had been recorded in full before setting it up for the next phase of the interview. She knew the recording would be essential to proving her case that Rue had a severe dissociative disorder and allow for a successful insanity defense if it ever came to a court or official hearing.

Almost an hour later, Rue awoke from her slightly drug-induced slumber. She sleepily acknowledged Colleen and asked how long she had been out.

"Almost two hours," replied the psychologist. "What do you recall before you fell asleep?"

Rue blinked hard in an attempt to return to the present.

"I remember talking about my mother's passing. Holding her hand. Seeing my dad…" she said sadly.

When prompted, Rue also recalled revisiting her husband's death with appropriate emotion. Colleen interpreted these recollections of the previous part of the session, that Rue was capable of opening up her subconscious and respond appropriately. It was time to dive deeper. Very deep.

In due course, Colleen mentioned Rue's sister Sophia.

"What do you recall doing with Sophia when you were a young child, around the age of five and six? What do you see if you close your eyes and go back to that time of your life?" suggested the psychologist.

"The first thing that comes to my mind is Sophia taking me shopping for some clothes. She loved doing that. I remember her taking me to Selfridge's on Oxford Street," Rue said with a smile.

"What do you remember about playing with Sophia?"

Rue broke into a soft smile.

"It was very cool. She handed down her many dolls and toys to me as she got older, and we would have fun playing with them. We shared the same room until I was about six."

The psychologist suggested that Rue imagine playing with those dolls and toys with Sophia.

"Can you see that?"

Rue smiled as she acknowledged the two girls playing in their bedroom.

Colleen was working her way to the exposure of traumatic memories with numerous questions. They might have seemed neutral to the ignorant onlooker, but the psychologist was diving down deeper into the iceberg.

"Do you remember the day Sophia got her driver's license?"

Rue's expression became stoically neutral.

"I think I was in school that day," she replied abruptly.

"Did you know that she was taking the test that day?"

"I don't remember."

"Did she drive much after she got her license?"

"Why are you asking me this?" said Rue tersely.

"Just relax, Rue," said Colleen supporting her suggestion with some relaxing rhythmic words.

After waiting a few minutes, Colleen continued.

"When Sophia was allowed out in the car, what did she drive?"

Another pause.

"She would drive my mother's car. It was a grey Toyota."

"Did you ever go with her, when Sophia drove your mum's car?" said the psychologist, stressing the name of her sister and using every opportunity to spark Rue's memory.

Rue's expression became increasingly unmoving, as if she was being drained of the life force. She sat silently and motionless, as if she were almost dead.

"Did Sophia ever take you for a ride into the countryside?" prompted Colleen.

A long silence and a confused look followed.

"I don't think so," said Rue eventually.

"I wonder whether Sophia would have ever taken you for a ride like, for example, when your parents weren't around," said the psychologist. "Like if they were on vacation or out of town."

"No, that would never happen!" said Rue in a desperate voice.

The iceberg was beginning to melt. It was something much more traumatic.

Suddenly, Rue emitted a horrific scream.

"NO! NO! NO!" She erupted, a desperate expulsion of unimaginable energy that had been buried beneath the surface for decades, burning her soul. The expression and ejection of the emotional lava buried the room in a torrent of torment and misery. She felt as if she had vomited up her very soul.

After what seemed like a decade to Rue, she collapsed into a sobbing testament to helplessness, a victim of evil.

Over the next hour, Colleen extracted the poison that had polluted Rue's mind-body since that fateful day in the English countryside.

Rue was able to recall all the aspects that her alter ego had previously made known to Colleen, and often with much more detail. Rue confirmed that the young men were unknown to them and that they never did tell anyone, until now.

After the revelation of the brutal rape, the memory of Sophia's death was much more easily remembered and processed. Rue admitted that she was not sure of what happened to her sister, especially now, in the light of her conscious awareness of what preceded her death. The memory previously had been hidden by the necessity to suffocate the truth.

The emotional hurricane that had ripped through Rue's soul, diminished into an occasional tornado, during which odd moments flashed into her now expanded consciousness.

At one point, Rue described some vague memories she had of going to Nat's room, where she found a very sad man asking to be put out of his misery.

"I can see me holding a pillow over his face, but I'm pretty sure he is close to death at this point. He's stopped breathing. I'm not getting anything else at the moment," she said almost apologetically.

"I didn't kill Nat did I?" Rue asked as a tornado formed right above her.

"No, you didn't kill Nat," said Colleen decisively. "He killed himself."

After spending quite some time, reassuring Rue and reflecting on her remarkable navigation of hell, Colleen ended the session.

"You have remarkably and courageously exorcised your demons, Rue. A new life is beginning."

Colleen then called in Julie the nurse and introduced her to Rue, explaining that she would be taking care of her needs and staying with her until the morning.

"A new day," said Colleen.

Chapter Thirty-Two

Friday: 9:00am

"You can search throughout the entire universe for someone who is more deserving of your love and affection than you are yourself, and that person is not to be found anywhere. You yourself, as much as anybody in the entire universe deserve your love and affection."
Buddha

The team met for their final official meeting with MI6. The only one missing was Rue, who was resting in her room under the watchful eyes of her capable nurse, Julie.

Jim was the first to speak.

"I want to thank each and every one of you here for graciously tolerating this difficult situation and helping us resolve the matter. I know it has not been easy, but with your help we have finally pieced the puzzle together."

"I especially want to acknowledge my colleague Colleen for working so diligently and brilliantly to clarify motives and solve the problem. Thank you, Colleen."

There was a raucous round of applause for the psychologist.

Colleen graciously acknowledged the appreciation as she stood up to speak.
"This whole episode has been about how we react to trauma. Many of us are fighting our own wars, that tear us apart. Nat didn't want

to live as a man who had contributed to thousands of deaths, and hopefully he is in a better place, one where these conflicts hopefully don't exist."

"Rue has begun to master her trauma and can now live her life, one that was strangled almost forty years ago, and is free. That's what freedom truly is, to be free of our demons."

"I'd now like to acknowledge our friends Sherlock Holmes and Dr. John Watson. Sherlock, your intuition about Rue and others, and your discovery of the pillow clue, was crucial to the investigation. Your stellar reputation has been maintained if not enhanced."

There was another round of applause, even from Dr. Rob.

Before there was any further discussion, the conference room door opened, and the team turned to see who was entering the room.

It was Rue.

She appeared simultaneously sad and buoyant.

Mary was sitting closest to Rue as she entered, and she stood up, walked slowly to greet Rue, reached out and hugged her tightly and silently. They both started to cry.

Before long there was a line of Rue's colleagues all waiting to express their love and compassion with long hugs that embraced Rue's soul. Holmes was even in the passionate queue. Sadness, grief, relief, and love cascaded down the walls of the majestic room.
After everyone had expressed their deep compassion, Mary asked Rue how she was feeling.

Rue paused.

"Right now, I'm feeling very loved," she said starting to tear up. "Thank you all. You don't know how much this means to me," she said stifling back more tears. "Thank you so much Colleen! You are my savior!"

"I am feeling many things. I am grieving my sister, my wonderful sister. I am grieving the loss my mother; I am grieving the loss of my husband. I am grieving the loss of my father; I am grieving the loss of our beloved friend Nat."

She paused once more to stifle the emotion that came from the feeling that in some way she had contributed to Nat's demise.

"I am very sad," she stopped once more to gulp down the sadness before continuing. "But I also feel free. Freer than I have ever been. I am ready to fly," she said stretching out her arms wide.

"I will no longer be weighed down by the trauma of the past. I will no longer think automatically and run from difficult feelings. Thank you!"

Rue smiled and then turned to Dr. Rob.

"I am no longer a robot, Rob!" she exclaimed to raucous applause. "My life is no longer stuck in regression analysis. I'm free to create the present. Now I can not just say but feel that my history is a teacher not a jailer.""

After the excited applause the room went quiet. There was nothing else to say. Then Sherlock stood up.

He addressed Rue.

"You are an extraordinarily brave and brilliant lady, Rue. I came here to prove that human intelligence is superior to artificial intelligence. However, I have been confronted with a different perception." The team waited to hear Holmes' insight.

"We are all robots. Our consciousness and the trillions of cells that are the subconscious, for one reason or another, often prevent us from seeing the truth. Whether that is because of tremendous trauma, such as Rue has experienced, or basic conditioning that we all face every minute of the day in today's world, we are not in control as much as we think we are. We have strong views and opinions that we never truly examine objectively, or even understand where they came from. We're on autopilot."

The assembled group nodded in assent.

"There's the difference between awareness and agency. Yes, we might be *aware* of events but that doesn't mean that we *control* them or our perceptions of them. Are we really any different from programmed robots?"

"Surely you're being a bit too pessimistic, Sherlock," suggested Shane.

"Well, there are things that can help us achieve true freedom, but we have to embrace them. Creativity and the ability – and willingness and courage – to see beyond not just the obvious but what we want to see. We must become open-minded and not stuck in confirmation bias. We must challenge everything, especially our own perceptions, and do so with respect. And we must embrace morality above all else. Without such actions, we are the ones with the artificial intelligence. This is the secret to wisdom. This is also the secret to true freedom as well as the secret to solving a complex crime."

"Unfortunately, however, I see how technology, and especially social media, is training us to lose our humanity. We are shown what our masters believe what we want to see through curated information, which erodes our ability to engage with the opposite. And virtual interaction is not the same as real life interaction. Is it
Dr. Watson?"

"No, it is not," said Watson. "There is now credible research that shows that when we are in virtual interaction our mirror neuron system that is responsible for being able to relate and identify with others, to train us to be compassionate and caring, does not work. It is interaction behind a wall that removes us from the necessity of being human."

Holmes picked up the argument from there.

"Imagine if that wonderful moment we just had with Rue was virtual and not real interaction. Would there have been the tears? Would there have been the delightful feelings of togetherness and compassion? Would it be the memorable moment that will live within us forever. Absolutely not."

Holmes paused to allow the team to reflect and feel the point.

"My friends, there's a difference between seeing a plane crash in front of your very eyes and watching a video of the same crash. We can be manipulated and lose our ability to be balanced and wise in the process. This blinkering works in two ways: It can inflate our ego or deflate it. That's what happened to Nat, as it has to many others. As brilliant as he was, he allowed the biased and distorted social media, including fake news, conspiracy theories and downright lies from our enemies, to reinforce his view that he was bad, no good, a loser. And it killed him. There is the real risk of automation and artificial intelligence."

***

The next few weeks proved crucial for everyone involved. As the Chinese economy did indeed collapse, the pressure applied by the allies eventually led to the end of conflict and a return to the negotiating table.

As a result of the de-escalation and eventual cessation of hostilities, the Bletchley team underwent a major transformation. Dr. Shane and Dr. Rob retained their roles. Earl left to resume his academic career as a professor at a major university, as did Mary. Ron retired after spending his entire career serving his country. Sandra, aka Karen, was given an assignment in an Interpol project and was now stationed in Paris.

Rue quit her job and planned a long period during which she would travel, reconnect with lost friends and relatives, enjoy her newfound freedom, and start living again. She also took up painting as her crushed creativity was splendidly reborn. Nat's tragedy was her resurrection.

Chapter Thirty-Three

***"I think and think for months and years. Ninety-nine
times, the conclusion is false. The hundredth time
I am right."***
Albert Einstein

A few weeks later, Sandra (aka Karen) returned from Europe and
planned a week's vacation in Bournemouth. Her parents had a
house by the waterfront which made an ideal getaway and Airbnb
location. Colleen found out she was coming to England, and the two
women arranged to meet. In fact, Colleen was delighted to not only
find out that Karen indeed was available but had also offered her a
room to stay in the house overnight. The two hadn't communicated
with each other at all since the resolution of Nat's demise.

Colleen arrived one Sunday afternoon, briefly unpacked and then
went out with her hostess to one of Karen's favorite eateries. The
food was enjoyable, and the conversation was about Colleen's latest
assignments, or at least as much as she could reveal.

Following a walk down by the beach after dinner the two former
colleagues retuned to Karen's place and relaxed with a delightful
glass of Pinot Grigio. In the secure privacy of Karen's vacation
home, the two ladies could finally relax and talk about what was on
both their minds.

"Well, my dear Colleen," Karen started, "your work at Bletchley was
simply amazing."

She raised her class, "Bien joue!"

Colleen smiled and thanked her for her plaudits.

Just then the doorbell rang. The women looked at each other inquisitively wondering who could possibly be at the house at this time of night. As Karen headed to the door, she looked down at the door cam video on her cellphone. There was a man standing there wearing a funny hat.

"Oh my God!" exclaimed Karen. "It's Holmes."

After a few seconds of dread, Colleen said, "Let him in. We need to know what he wants."

Trying to conceal her panic, Karen opened the door.

"Mr. Holmes, what an unexpected pleasure to see ya," greeted Karen.

"I apologize for interrupting you so late at night, but might I come in and talk with you. I believe Colleen is here, too, is she not?"

"Yeh, er, um, she is…" stuttered Karen.

Holmes entered and acknowledged Colleen with a smile.

Colleen forced a return smile at Holmes before asking about Dr. Watson.

"Dr. Watson is fine but no, he's not here. There are some things that even he cannot be privy to," said Holmes.

"Would you like some vino, Mr. Holmes?" Karen offered, trying hard to present her usual cool demeanor.

"No thank you," Holmes responded before asking, "Should I call you Sandra or Karen?"

"Whichever you wish, Mr. Holmes."

"Rest assured ladies there will be no consequences for what I am about to reveal. I just want you to know that I was not misled and perhaps my observations can help you in your future assignments."

Karen felt relieved, Colleen was fascinated. Both had a sense that Holmes was about to tell them a new version of the truth.

"As you revealed a few weeks ago at the Range, Rue and specifically her alter ego ensured Nat's death. However, you missed out one important detail," he said to Colleen.

Karen looked on in horror as she waited for Holmes' proclamation. Colleen didn't have any idea what he was talking about.

"Sandra, you instigated the murder by manipulating Rue and her especially her alter ego," declared Holmes.

The two women froze as Holmes continued.

"It has been apparent to me for some time that you, Sandra, are the protagonist in this case. You lied to us about your previous experiences, and I knew watching you in the bunker during the drone attack that you were used to be being in similar traumatic situations. I also know that it was you who acquired the strychnine and ensured that Nat knew where it was stored. I also know that there were no rodents in the kitchen or anywhere else inside the Range."

The two women said nothing and let Holmes continue.

"The only feasible conclusion is that you were acting as a government agent. So, why would the government want to remove Nat? Obviously, he was a threat of some sort. Which brings us to the timing of his murder. Why would he die immediately after he had helped his country achieve a major victory and effectively turn the tide of the war? By all accounts Nat was not very happy with the outcome of his plan. That's probably because it wasn't his plan, and it was not an outcome that he wanted. Which suggests the main motive in this matter; that Nat was secretly working for or with the Chinese."

Karen and Colleen were stunned into silence by both Holmes' insight and its possible implications.

However, Holmes wasn't finished.

"I have to say it was a brilliant move exploiting Rue's dissociation and getting her, or rather her male alter ego, to commit the crime."

"Colleen you probably don't know this. Have you ever met Dr. Gabrielle Fulmer?" continued Holmes.

"I know she has worked at the department before I did but I have never met her. What has she got to do with all this?" asked Colleen.

"Well, the official records show that all of those working at the Range underwent a psychological evaluation before being hired.
They were all conducted by a Gracie Parker."

"Oh, yes, I knew that. I know Gracie and her mother Ann pretty well," said Colleen.

"I used my technological skills to explore the dark web and decode the official electronic records and found out something interesting," continued Holmes.

"Wait a minute!" said Karen angrily. "You made it clear to us that you were very anti-tech and didn't have a damn clue about it!"

"Sandra, you should always question what people tell you and why you should or shouldn't believe them."

Colleen wondered why Karen was so worked up.

"Colleen, I found out that Rue had an additional six sessions with another psychologist that weren't part of the official record."

"That's downright illegal Holmes!" shouted Karen.

"Please continue, Sherlock," said Colleen overriding Karen's obvious objections.

"The sessions were all with Gabrielle Fulmer. Further research showed that Dr. Fulmer is an expert in hypnosis and dissociative disorder."

Karen chugged down the remainder of her glass of wine and quickly poured herself another one.

"What are you saying, Sherlock?" asked Colleen.

"MI6 knew about Rue's dissociation. However, Dr. Fulmer's involvement was to help them understand her psyche and evaluate her safety. I am assuming that after the work with Dr. Fulmer they realized that Rue's condition was exactly what made her a great candidate for the job. It made her incredibly focused and amazingly productive. Dr. Fulmer's sessions were not about helping Rue rid herself of her demons but keeping them in place."

"Is this true, Karen?" asked Colleen incredulously.

Karen didn't reply but took another large gulp of wine.

"I believe that these sessions with Dr. Fulmer were focused more on conversations with her male alter ego, the 'doctor' and that they weren't discussed with Rue herself. There was no need to do that, in fact, to the contrary, that would have been counterproductive."

"I also suspect that Rue's condition was one of the main reasons why Sandra was assigned to the Range. Someone needed to be there who understand the reality of Rue's psyche," said Holmes.

Colleen looked at Karen again. This time Karen returned a submissive look. She, or the wine, had obviously managed to assert some control over her initial anger.

"Then, this difficult situation with Nat arose. Someone, possibly Sandra, came up with the clever idea of accessing the 'doctor' and engaging him to go to Nat's room and ensure he didn't live," Holmes said.

Colleen's eyes widened as she realized the implication of what Holmes was about to reveal.

"Someone, and I am guessing it was Sandra, called Dr. Fulmer and got her to access the 'doctor' and instructed him to carry out what was necessary."

"Someone also arranged for the technical operatives at MI6 to eradicate all the phone calls during the critical time period, to cover up any evidence of Dr. Fulmer's call to Rue and the 'doctor'. I was able to establish that there was just one call during the time period in question, which I believe was Dr. Fulmer's call to Rue."

"Is this true?" Colleen demanded of Karen.

"Yes, it is," affirmed Karen before continuing, "So, what do you intend to do with this information, Holmes?"

"Why nothing, of course. I wouldn't stand in the way of the government doing what is needed at a time of war, nor would it be of any advantage to me to do so. However, Karen, please be careful. You must always act your role and stay in character. It was the bunker experience that got me exploring your real identity and possible role in the entire fiasco. I know it wasn't your fault that Ron was informed of the previous engagement with the meth lab but that was also another clue. And lastly, it didn't take much to get us to learn from Aram at the exterminators about the strychnine. That should have remained a total secret. And you made sure that Nat knew where the strychnine was."

"You're completely right Holmes," said Karen. "I have definitely learned from this whole fiasco."

Karen then recounted some of the events.

"When MI6 found out that Nat was more interested in artificial intelligence than patriotism, we thought of many ways he could be removed. But the way it ended seemed perfect," said Karen.

"How long did you know that Nat was passing technology information to the Chinese?" asked Holmes.

"There had been suspicion for some time. That's when we decided to ask him to come up with a plan to trap the enemy. Naturally, he frickin' stalled, which increased our suspicions. The plan he submitted was, of course, changed and he was told that we weren't going to implement it. Then we acted immediately and caught the Chinese and Nat completely off guard. Once the plan had been successfully implemented Nat knew his time was up. You might recall me telling you that he was less than happy when the news broke."

Karen continued.

"Of course, I had already made sure that he had got some strychnine the day before. We had also ensured that Nat got a message supposedly from the Chinese, furious at his actions, that the gig was up, and he was a dead man walking. That set him up for his perceived suicide attempt."

She continued, "I kept Gabrielle informed and called her that evening and explained what was happening and that she needed to get Rue – and the 'doctor' -- to go into Nat's room around midnight, stimulate her alter ego to apply the strychnine if he hadn't already done so."

"We were monitoring his room, knew that he was restless but hadn't made any suicidal moves yet and that's when I explained what Gabrielle had to do immediately. She did her thing because we couldn't let him live a second longer. We simply couldn't wait for him to take enough of the poison himself. That might have taken another hour or two and who knows what havoc he would have created in that time with calls and notes and reaching out to the press, and that sort of thing. Gabrielle did a great job getting the "doctor" to suffocate him and ensure the poison evidence was in place. Made it convincingly look like suicide. A genuine motive and the ideal weapon.”

“I can’t help feeling more than a bit betrayed,” said Colleen solemnly. “Why didn’t you tell me, Karen?”

“I wanted to, but obviously I couldn’t. I wanted you to help Rue recover and give her proper therapy not bloody use her. And we needed those sessions on the record to prove that Rue didn’t know what was happening and not responsible. Please forgive me,” Karen implored.

“Colleen your colleague here was put in a difficult position and handled it the best she could under the difficult circumstances,” said Holmes.

After a short pause Colleen got up from her seat, walked over to Karen and reached down to give her a hug.

“Nobody ever said this job would ever be easy,” reflected Colleen before she and Karen gripped each other tighter before releasing themselves.

Colleen commented, “Well, fortunately or otherwise, people with dissociative disorder are very easily manipulated once you know how their psyche is organized. I am sure that Gabrielle had already created and used the exact words that would activate ‘the doctor’.”

“How is Rue doing now?” asked Holmes.

“Well, her relief at remembering and resolving the rape has been liberating and she knows that the “doctor” ensured Nat’s death, so she is doing much better. I have been working with her and guiding her and I don’t think the reality of Gabrielle directing her alter ego will ever come into the light of her consciousness. In fact, she is travelling in America right now," said Colleen.

Holmes stood up.

"Well, my dear ladies, I won't bother you any more about this incident. Hopefully, it has been a lesson for all of us. I can assure you this information will never be revealed by me. And if you ever need any assistance in matters like this, I would be delighted to help you again."

About Howard J. Rankin PhD

Dr. Howard Rankin has extensive expertise and knowledge in the areas of psychology, neuroscience, and behavior change. He is a storyteller and a best-selling and award-winning author. Dr. Rankin has written twelve books in his own name, co-written another twelve, and ghostwritten thirty others, all nonfiction. This book is his first novel. Howard has also published more than thirty scientific articles on addiction and behavior change and has been a consultant to the NIH and WHO as well as editor of a major psychological journal. His work in psychology and his writing have been featured in many newspapers and magazines and he has appeared on national networks including CNN, ABC, CBS, BBC, as well as on "The View" and "20/20."

His latest books include *I Think Therefore I Am Wrong: A Guide to Bias, Political Correctness, Fake News and the Future of Mankind*, which explores the default setting of the mind and how that can lead us astray, and *Power Talk: The Art of Effective Communication* and *Intuitive Rationality: The new behavioral direction of AI* with Grant Renier. *Falling to Grace: The Art and Science of Redemption*, was released on April 15, 2022, and was featured in *Psychology Today* (May 2022). He is also the presenter of *How Not to Think about Health and Wellbeing* on the UK Health Radio network.

Howard is also a *Psychology Today* blogger, the creator and host of the *How Not To Think* podcast, and Science Director at IntualityAI. Currently one of his books, *The Journey of the All-American Red Heads*, is being made into a documentary, with the possibility of it being also made into a movie. He is currently creating a presentation and book about the mind-body theory called *The Miracle Within You.*

Social media

http://www.beempoweredbyhoward.com/

http://www.drhowardjrankin.com/

https://www.facebook.com/howard.rankin.7/

https://www.linkedin.com/in/drhrankinthecommunicator/

https://www.instagram.com/drhrankin/

https://twitter.com/howard_rankin

https://www.tiktok.com/@howardrankin1?lang=en

About Intualityai

Intuality AI is an artificial intelligence company empowering people by identifying actionable future events. We show you the future by predicting near-term and far-future events from streams of realtime data and providing directive alerts about critical events to make better decisions.

For more information, visit http://www.intualityai.com/

Some Other Books by Howard

Intuitive Rationality: The New Behavioral Direction of AI
Grant Renier and Howard Rankin 2021
https://bit.ly/44bHnNI

Falling to Grace: The Art and Science of Redemption
https://amzn.to/35f0xKe

I Think Therefore I am Wrong: A Guide to Bias, Political
Correctness, Fake News and the Future of Mankind
https://amzn.to/2tMLDrX

Power Talk: The Art of Effective Communication
https://amzn.to/45thxWz

If you enjoyed this book, please feel free to provide a review on
Amazon or other bookseller sites.

Sources

Pert, Candace. *Molecules of Emotion*. 1999. Simon and Schuster

Lieff, John. *The Secret Language of Cells: What Biological Conversations Tell Us About the Brain-Body Connection, the Future of Medicine, and Life Itself.* 2020. Benbella Books.

Daniel Kahneman. *Thinking, Fast and Slow.* 2013. Farrar, Straus and Giroux.

Hubert Dreyfus. *Why Computers Must Have Bodies in Order to be Intelligent.* 1967. The Review of Metaphysics Vol. 21, No. 1 (Sep., 1967), pp. 13-32

Jakub Schimmelpfennig, Jan Topczewski, Wojciech Zajkowski, and Kamila Jankowiak-Siuda. *The role of the salience network in cognitive and affective deficits.* Front. Hum. Neurosci., 20 March 2023.

page 86
Spurious correlations
https://www.tylervigen.com/spurious-correlations

Page 99
"Any girl can be glamorous; all you have to do is stand still and look stupid," attributed to Hedy Lamarr.

Page 105
"Sometimes it is the people no one imagines anything of who do the things that no one can imagine," attributed to Alan Turing.

New Study Links Brain Injuries to "Acquired Sociopathy". Big Think, December 2017.

https://bigthink.com/surprising-science/these-types-of-headinjuries-could-increase-your-risk-of-committing-a-crime/#:~:text=Other%20serial%20killers%20had%20suffered,Gary%20Heidnik%2C%20and%20Ed%20Gein.

History of Violence Against LGBT People in the United States. Wikipedia.
https://en.wikipedia.org/wiki/History_of_violence_against_LGBT_people_in_the_United_States

Sumter, M., Wood, F., Whitaker, I., & Berger-Hill, D. *Religion and Crime studies: Assessing what has been learned. religions,* 9(6), 193. doi:10.3390/rel9060193. 2018)

Caldwell, M., Andrews, J.T.A., Tanay, T. et al. AI-enabled Future Crime. Crime Sci 9, 14 (2020). https://doi.org/10.1186/s40163020-00123-8

Page 110
Daniel Kish
https://en.wikipedia.org/wiki/Daniel_Kish

Page 111
Akira Haraguchi digit recall
https://en.wikipedia.org/wiki/Akira_Haraguchi#:~:text=Haraguchi%20holds%20the%20current%20unofficial,a.m.%20on%20October%204%2C%202006.

Page 112
Timur Gareyev, blindfolded chess games
https://www.grunge.com/105691/record-breaking-mental-featsblew-everyone-away/

Insanity defense
https://www.law.cornell.edu/wex/insanity_defense

Newson JJ, Pastukh V, Sukhoi O, Taylor J and Thiagarajan TC, Mental State of the World 2020, Sapien Labs, March 2021
https://www.mentalstateoftheworld.report/msw-2021/

www.ingramcontent.com/pod-product-compliance
Lightning Source LLC
Chambersburg PA
CBHW071307140726
47996CB00005B/1666